THE CONCEPT
OF MOTIVATION

by

R. S. PETERS

LONDON

ROUTLEDGE & KEGAN PAUL

NEW YORK: HUMANITIES PRESS

First published in England 1958
by Routledge & Kegan Paul Ltd
Broadway House, 68-74 Carter Lane
London, E.C.4

Second edition 1960

Reprinted 1963, 1965, 1967
Printed in Great Britain
by Lowe & Brydone (Printers) Ltd
London, N.W.10

CONTENTS

ACKNOWLEDGMENTS

MY thanks are due to Miss P. Bourne and to Mrs. V. Carver for typing the MS., to Henri Tajfel for making some comments on the exposition of drive theories, to Dr. Ernest Jones who made some comments on the chapter on Freud's theory and to my colleague, David Hamlyn, who discussed many of the conceptual points with me and who made acute and painstaking comments on the completed MS. My thanks are also due to Professor C. A. Mace, head of the department of psychology at Birkbeck College, whose detailed constructive comments on the monograph convinced me that he should really have written it himself.

Birkbeck College,
Malet Street, W.C.1.
July 1957

PREFACE TO SECOND EDITION

MINOR changes have been made in this edition, mainly in Ch. IV, in order to safeguard the argument against further misunderstanding. I am indebted to my colleague, Harry Hurwitz, and to Alan Watson, who were critical of my thesis about 'drives'. Both went to much trouble to indicate to me where such misunderstandings might arise, and where my thesis is most open to criticism. My thanks are overdue to my colleague,

A. P. Griffiths, who helped me to get clearer about the thesis of my original *Philosophy* paper [on which Ch. II was based], that 'motives' are a *special class* of reasons for action, and to A. R. White, whose paper 'The Language of Motives', *Mind*, 67, 1958 (which he sent for my comments before publication), also helped me to make my thesis more explicit.

Some psychologists have praised the Monograph for discussing psychological explanations with much more knowledge of theories actually advanced by psychologists than is usual with philosophical critics of psychology. But they have suggested that I have taken such theories too seriously! They are to be seen as moves in a game, not as *ex cathedra* pronouncements. I am well aware that psychologists are now very critical of ambitious theories like those of Freud and Hull and that these have been replaced by a bewildering amount of piecemeal theorizing that it would be impossible to deal with in a Monograph that is already too long. But I think that these theories are still very influential. For though they are outmoded as Grand Plans, their concepts still persist in the fragments of their monolithic structures. And the new piecemeal theories, because they employ many of the old concepts, still carry with them many of the more general and more unacceptable implications of the ambitious theories in which these concepts had a natural home. Hence the concentration on concepts and on the classical theories.

Birkbeck College,
Malet Street, W.C.1.
October 1959

CHAPTER ONE

TYPES OF EXPLANATION IN PSYCHOLOGICAL THEORIES

'Whether a given proposition is true or false, significant or meaningless, depends upon what questions it was meant to answer.'   R. G. COLLINGWOOD

Introductory

EVER since Hobbes was fired by the imaginative idea that *all* human behaviour might be explained in terms of mechanical principles, there have been sporadic attempts to provide over-all theories of human behaviour. Such theories have been instigated more by the desire to develop an ambitious theory than by puzzlement about concrete problems of human behaviour. This was true of Hobbes who pictured himself doing for psychology what Harvey had done for physiology by extending the new science of motion to the most intimate spheres of human thought and endeavour. It was also true of later theorists who, under the influence of Darwin rather than of Galileo, were excited by the thought that men were animals as well as mere bodies. McDougall, for instance, did not provide any startling answers to concrete questions about human behaviour; rather he concocted a sort of dynamic atomism to show that

1

man's social behaviour could be explained in terms of biological principles. In fact the inspiration behind theorizing in psychology has been, in the main, the success of other sciences like physiology, chemistry, and mechanics, and the idea that there could be an all-inclusive theory of human behaviour if psychology were to adopt the postulates and methods of other sciences.

A contributory factor, too, has been the understandable determination of psychologists to make their enquiries 'scientific'. This has led them to cast their theories in a mould dictated by the current conception of scientific method. For a long time this was thought to be the method of induction; and so systems of psychology like introspectionism and behaviourism, developed, which were products of what Popper calls 'inductivism'—attempts to build up generalisations on the basis of carefully scrutinized data. (Peters, 1951). The methodologists then proclaimed that scientific method was really deductive. So an enormity like Hull's *Principles of Behaviour* emerged, scientifically impeccable because it was a hypothetico-deductive system. Hull (1943) boldly proclaimed his programme of starting from 'colourless movements and mere receptor impulses as such' and eventually explaining everything in terms of such concepts—

> 'familial behaviour, individual adaptive efficiency (intelligence), the formal educative processes, psychogenic disorders, social control and delinquency, character and personality, culture and acculturation, magic and religious practices, custom law and jurisprudence, politics and government and many other specialised fields of behaviour.'

In fact Hull developed some simple postulates which gave dubious answers to limited questions about particular species of rats. He never asked, let alone tried to answer, any concrete questions about human behaviour. He was in love with the idea of a science of behaviour; he was not acutely worried about concrete questions of explaining *human* behaviour.

Freud was perhaps the great exception. For he was genuinely puzzled about concrete phenomena and developed some very fertile assumptions to explain them. Also, in his early work especially, he was very much aware of the limitations of his assumptions and defined carefully the types of phenomena that could be explained by the postulation of unconscious mental processes. In other words he seemed to be aware of the *sort* of questions about human behaviour which he was answering. For there are many *different* sorts of questions which can be asked about human behaviour and the differences, as I shall hope to show, are such that an all-embracing theory is inappropriate. These different sorts of questions are especially confused in theories of motivation. It is this thesis which I now hope to substantiate.

I *Types of questions about human behaviour*

(*a*) 'HIS REASON' EXPLANATIONS. The over-riding aim of a scientist should be explanation. This sounds rather obvious, but it has many important consequences in relation to psychological theorizing. For the general question 'Why did Jones do that?' is capable of being asked and answered in a variety of different ways. The particular formula employed in asking the question usually dictates the sort of answer

which is expected and which counts as an explanation.[1]
The paradigm case of a human action is when something is done in order to bring about an end. So the
usual way of explaining an action is to describe it as
an action of a certain sort by indicating the end which
Jones had in mind. We therefore ask the 'why'
question in a more specific form. We ask what was
his *reason* for doing that or what was the *point* of it,
what *end* he had in mind. If we ask why Jones walked
across the road, the obvious answer will be something
like 'To buy tobacco.' Instead of saying this we could
say 'because he wanted some tobacco'. This is,
logically speaking, another way of giving the same
sort of answer; for the answer 'to buy some tobacco'
is only an explanation because we assume in Jones
some sort of directive disposition—a general tendency
to obtain and use tobacco (Peters, 1952).

Even in this very simple sort of explanation in
terms of a man's reason for doing something there are,
as a matter of fact, concealed assumptions. We
assume, for instance, that walking across the street
is an efficient way of getting to the tobacconist. This
counts as an explanation not simply because Jones
envisaged walking across the street as a means to
getting the tobacco but because it really is a means to
getting it. We assume, too, that a man who has this
information will act on it if he wants some tobacco.
We assume that men are rational in that they will
take means which lead to ends if they have the information and want the ends. 'His reason' is an
explanation in terms of what Popper (1945) calls
'the logic of the situation'.

[1] I am indebted to J. O. Urmson (1952) for some of these distinctions.

But it is not only norms of efficiency and consistency that are implicit in the concept of 'his reason'. There are also norms or standards of social appropriateness. After all Jones might have crawled or run across the road. But 'to get some tobacco' would be a very odd answer to the question 'Why did Jones *run* across the road?' Yet running would be quite an efficient way of getting across the road. It would, however, be socially odd as a way of crossing the road to get some tobacco. *Man is a rule-following animal.* His actions are not simply directed towards ends; they also conform to social standards and conventions, and unlike a calculating machine he acts because of his knowledge of rules and objectives. For instance, we ascribe to people *traits* of character like honesty, punctuality, considerateness and meanness. Such terms do not, like ambition or hunger or sexual desire, indicate the sorts of goals that a man tends to pursue; rather they indicate the type of regulation that he imposes on his conduct whatever his goals may be. A man who is ruthless, selfish, punctual, considerate, persistent, and honest, does not have any particular goals; rather he pursues whatever goals he has in particular sorts of ways.

This simple purposive model of a man taking means to bring about an end is further complicated by the fact that norms enter into and often entirely define the end. Ends like passing an examination, getting married, becoming a professor, and reading a paper, explain quite adequately a great deal of the goings on in the precincts of a university; yet they are defined almost entirely by social convention. It is a gross over-simplification to think of ends merely as terminating points of activity. Actually even a rat, after eating or achieving some other end, will continue being active in a variety of ways—sniffing, preening, and so on. If eating can be regarded as an end this is not because it is a definite terminating point of activity but because activity *previous* to it varies concomitantly with changes in the conditions necessary to define it as an end. The concept of means is just as necessary to bring out what is meant by an end as the concept of end is to bring out what is meant by a means. Ends are not given as natural terminating points like a chain of oases distributed across a desert. And, to a large extent, what counts as falling within a means-to-end explanatory framework is determined by convention. Even those ends, like eating and sexual intercourse, which are universal and which have an obvious biological basis, can scarcely be specified without recourse to norms. For there are countless ways of performing the acts which can be regarded as ends and in every culture a few particular ways are stamped with the hallmark of conventionality. Eating is not just getting food into the stomach. Jones' movements across the road are classifiable as means to the end of buying tobacco because of a vast system of norms defining 'buying tobacco' as an end as well as a system of norms regulating what is an efficient and socially appropriate way of attaining it.

My reasons for stressing this rule-following purposive pattern into which we fit our common-sense explanations are twofold. In the first place I want to insist that most of our explanations are couched in terms of this model and our predictions of people's behaviour presuppose it. We know what the parson will do when he begins to walk towards the pulpit because we know the conventions regulating church services. And we can make such predictions without knowing anything about the *causes* of people's behaviour unless we include under 'causes' things like the parson's training and grasp of the rules, which are things of a different order from 'causes' in the sense of antecedent movements. Man in society is like a chess-player writ large. Requests for explanation are usually reflections of our ignorance about the particular rule or goal which is relevant to the behaviour in question. We usually know the general pattern but are unsure which part of it is relevant. Sometimes, of course, we are in the position of a free-thinker at a Roman Catholic mass. The question 'Why did X do that?' is then usually a request for an elucidation of the whole pattern of conventions. In explaining human actions we, like anthropologists, must all, in the first place be structuralists. Indeed I would go so far as to say that anthropology or sociology must be the basic sciences of human action in that they exhibit the systematic framework of norms and goals which are necessary to classify actions as being of a certain sort. They both—like classical economics—presuppose the purposive, rule-following model; in this respect they are quite unlike sciences which imply a mechanical model of explanation.

In the second place this rule-following purposive pattern of explanation must be sketched in some detail because a proper understanding of what is meant by a human action has very important logical consequences. It shows, for instance, as I shall argue, that human actions cannot be sufficiently explained in terms of causal concepts like 'colourless movements'. Indeed to claim that we are confronted with an action is *ipso facto* to rule out such mechanical explanations, as being sufficient.

(B) 'THE REASON' EXPLANATIONS. But, of course, as psychologists will be the first to point out, people often invent reasons for doing things or delude themselves into thinking that the reasons they offer for their actions are operative reasons. We therefore often say of a man that *his* reason may have been x but *the* reason why he acted like that was y. For instance we might say that Jones said that he crossed the road in order to buy some tobacco but the reason why he did it was not really his desire for tobacco; it was sex. There was a pretty girl looking in the window of the tobacconist. This explanation may of course be erroneous. For instance a psychologist once told me that I delayed crossing the road to College because of an aversion to getting down to work. I replied, and I think more convincingly, that I stayed on the other side in order to look at the row of glistening cars drawn up opposite. But whether the explanation in question is correct or incorrect does not much matter ; the point is that to speak of *the* reason why a person does something is different in that it is a way of calling attention to the law or assumed law that a given case actually falls under. *His* reason may coincide with *the* reason. *The* reason why Jones crossed the road might in fact be his desire for tobacco. He might also be aware that he wanted to inspect the girl at close quarters, but was concealing this by the camouflage of buying tobacco. This would then be his *real* reason.

But whereas *his* reason—whether real or not—entails that a man is conscious of his objective, the reason why he did it does not.[1] *The* reason why he did it might well be sex or aversion to work; yet the individual might be quite unaware of pursuing or avoiding the relevant goals. And whereas to say that *he* had a reason for doing something is more or less to rule out a causal explanation, to give *the* reason why he did it is sometimes to subsume it under a law-like proposition of a causal kind. This is not necessarily so. For we can say that sex or aversion to work was *the* reason why he did it and simply be insisting that a different directive disposition is being exercised. But *the* reason why he did it might also be that he was pushed or assailed by an attack of giddiness. These would be causal explanations which would rebut the suggestion that he had a reason for crossing the road. Causal explanations, in other words, can count as *the* reason why a person does something; but they are only one type of answer to the question 'What was *the* reason why he did it?'

(c) CAUSAL EXPLANATIONS. There are, however, other questions about particular goings on—I omit to say actions on purpose—to which answers in causal terms are appropriate. Instead of the omnibus

[1] Hamlyn has pointed out to me the use of "the reason for his action" as well as "the reason why he did it". "The reason for" seems to be similar to "his reason" but to imply a coincidence between "his reason" and "the reason why he did it". I am not here concerned with the use of "reason" in the context of *justification* as when we say that a reason for giving up smoking is that it causes lung cancer. "His reason" and "the reason for" can be used in contexts both of justification and of explanation. Needless to say "the reason why he did it" is reserved for contexts of explanation with which I am here concerned.

B

question 'Why did Jones do that?' we often ask what made, drove, or possessed him to do it. These are usually cases of lapses from action or failure to act—when there is some kind of *deviation* from the purposive rule-following model, when people, as it were, get it wrong. This may be in respect of an efficiency norm—for example, when a person refuses to take the only quick route to his destination by underground train, or when he can't remember a well-known name when he is performing an introduction. Or the behaviour may go wrong in respect of a norm governing social appropriateness—as with a business man who runs to work when he is not late or a tutor who crawls round the room sniffing while listening to an undergraduate essay. Or behaviour may go wrong by being deflected towards a peculiar goal as with a married man who suddenly makes an advance to a choir boy. In such cases it is as if the man suffers something rather than does something. It is because things seem to be happening to him that it is appropriate to ask what made, drove, or possessed him to do that. The appropriate answer in such cases may be in terms of a causal theory

These cases of particular goings on which look like breakdowns of action are very similar to a whole class of general activities which seem to have no point or a very odd point—dreams, hallucinations, obsessions, anxieties and perversions. In such cases the Greeks suggested that the gods intervene and take possession of the individual's mind. Very often recourse is made to crude physiological explanations. It was not till the advent of Freud that any systematic explanation of such goings-on was offered in psychological terms. Indeed Freud claimed in 1913 that the main contribution of psycho-analysis to general psychology was to link together and to give psychological explanations for happenings which had previously been left to physiology or to folk-lore. Many have claimed that Freud, by reclaiming these phenomena for psychology, was in fact extending the model of purposive rule-following behaviour to cover the unconscious. He showed, it is argued, that we have reasons for acts which were previously only explained in terms of causes. I shall argue later that this thesis is mistaken. Freud showed, perhaps, that the concept of 'wish' has a wider application than was previously thought. But his account of the working of the primary processes creaks with causality. In maintaining that in the unconscious there is no sense of causal or logical connexion he was *ipso facto* denying that the model of 'his reason', implying norms of efficiency and social appropriateness, was relevant. Freud, I shall argue, provides the classic case of giving quasi-causal explanations where causal explanations seem *prima facie* appropriate.

I shall also argue that Freud in fact only intended to explain by reference to unconscious mental processes cases where the purposive rule-following model breaks down or is inappropriate. He did not think— and often explicitly denied— that this sort of explanation can be appropriately given for everything —for cases where a man acts as well as for cases where something happens to a man. In this respect Freud was, from the point of view of my argument, on the side of the angels. For my case is not simply that causal explanations are otiose when we know the point of a person's action in that, life being short and time

limited, we no longer feel inclined to ask 'why' once
we have accommodated a piece of behaviour within
the rule-following purposive model. It is also that if
we are in fact confronted with a case of a genuine
action (i.e. an act of doing something as opposed to
suffering something), then causal explanations are
ipso facto inappropriate as sufficient explanations.
Indeed they may rule out rule-following purposive
explanations. To ask what made Jones do something
is at least to suggest that he had no good reason for
doing it. Similarly to ascribe a point to his action is
ipso facto to deny that it can be *sufficiently explained*
in terms of causes, though, of course, there will be
many causes in the sense of *necessary* conditions. A
story can always be told about the underlying mechanisms; but this does not add up to a sufficient explanation, if it is an action that has to be explained.

To give a causal *explanation* of an event involves at
least showing that other conditions being presumed
unchanged a change in one variable is a *sufficient*
condition for a change in another. In the mechanical
conception of 'cause' it is also demanded that there
should be spatial and temporal contiguity between
the movements involved. Now the trouble about
giving this sort of explanation of human actions is
that we can never specify an action exhaustively in
terms of movements of the body or within the body.
(Hamlyn, 1953.) It is therefore impossible to state
sufficient conditions in terms of antecedent movements which may vary concomitantly with subsequent movements. 'Signing a contract', for instance,
is a typical example of a human action. The movements involved are grouped together because they are

seen by the agent to be efficient and appropriate means to an end. But it would be impossible to stipulate exhaustively what the movements *must* be. For if this is a case of a human action the agent must be presumed to be intelligent and he will, accordingly, vary his movements in a great variety of ways. He may hold the pen slightly differently, vary the size of his writing according to the space available, and so on, depending on the sort of ink, paper, and pen available. But provided that he produces a signature which confirms to rough and ready criteria—e.g., it must not be typed—more or less *any* movements will do. I suppose he could sign a contract by holding the pen between his toes. A very general range of movements could perhaps be specified, but no specific movements of the muscles, limbs, or nervous system, which *must* occur before it would be conceded that a contract had been signed. This is tantamount to saying that the concept of an action is inseparable from that of intelligence; for part of what we mean by 'intelligence' is the ability to vary movements relative to a goal in a way which is appropriate to changes in the situation necessary to define it as a goal and in the conditions relevant to attaining it. So we could never give a sufficient explanation of an action in causal terms because we could never stipulate the movements which would have to count as dependent variables. A precise functional relationship could never be established. Of course, just as we could stipulate a general range of movements necessary to define signing a contract, so also we could lay down certain very general *necessary* conditions. We could, for instance, say that a man could not sign a contract unless he had a brain and nervous system. Such physiological knowledge *might* enable us to predict *bodily movements*. And *if* we had bridging laws to correlate such physiological findings with descriptions of actions we might *indirectly predict* actions. But we would *first* have to grasp concepts connected with action like 'knowing what we are doing' and 'grasp of means to an end'. As such concepts have no application at the level of mere movement, such predictions would not count as sufficient *explanations* of *actions*.

Furthermore, as I have already argued, general standards or rules are implicit in the concept of an action. We can therefore say that a man is doing something efficiently, correctly, and so on, if he knowingly varies what he does in accordance with changes in the situation conventionally singled out as the goal and the conditions perceived as relevant to attaining it. It only makes sense to talk of actions in this way, not of cases where something happens to a man. A man's action may break down because of a causal condition like a lesion in his brain. But all that can be said of such causal conditions is that they just occur. Movements *qua* movements are neither intelligent, efficient, nor correct. They only become so in the context of an action. There cannot therefore be a sufficient explanation of actions in causal terms because, as Popper has put it, there is a logical gulf between nature and convention. Statements implying norms and standards cannot be deduced from statements about mere movements which have no such normative implications. The contention that man is a rule-following animal must, if taken seriously, entail that the transition from nature to convention occurs whenever we try to give a sufficient explanation of human actions in causal terms. There is, however, no objection to such explanations of what *happens* to a man; for happenings cannot be characterized as intelligent or unintelligent, correct or incorrect, efficient or inefficient. *Prima facie* they are just occurrences. Perhaps Freud showed that some lapses and breakdowns may not be *just* occurrences. But this is another story. The point is that there is a *prima facie* case for treating them as such.

To make explicit the implications of my thesis for psychological theories : If the question is 'Why did Jones walk across the road?' a *sufficient* explanation can only be given in terms of the rule-following purposive model—if this is a case of an action rather than of something happening to him. Answers in terms of causal concepts like 'receptor impulses' and 'colourless movement', are either not explanations because they state not sufficient but only necessary conditions, or they are ways of denying that what has to be explained is a human action. If we ask 'Why did Jones *jump* while he was crossing the road?' it might be appropriate to say 'because of a twinge in his stomach' or 'because a car back-fired'. The stimulus-response sort of model would perhaps be appropriate and the causal type of explanation in terms of internal or external stimulation might be sufficient because the assumption might be that Jones was suffering something rather than performing an action. This sort of jump would then be quite different from the jump he might perform while competing in an athletic contest.

This is not to deny that causal explanations are

relevant to human actions. It is only to deny that they are sufficient explanations of them. Causal theories have at least three jobs to do in this context. Firstly they can state *necessary* conditions for human actions to occur. Hebb's physiological speculations, for instance, might well provide a sketch of a typical class of necessary conditions. But this does not mean that such speculations *explain* human actions. Secondly, as a corollary, they could show that some individual differences in performance are dependent on slight differences in such necessary conditions. Hebb's hypothesis of the relationship between the size of the association areas of the brain and the possibility of late learning would be such a hypothesis. Thirdly such theories could be used to give *sufficient* conditions for breakdowns in performance, as in the case of brain lesions, by indicating a necessary condition which was absent. Alternatively lapses and breakdowns could be explained by the postulation of special disrupting conditions—e.g. Freud's theory of the unconscious wish.

(D) END-STATE EXPLANATIONS. There are, of course, all sorts of higher level questions which can be asked about human actions, most of which are irrelevant to psychology in general and theories of motivation in particular. Questions, for instance, can be raised about the conventions in accordance with which a man acts or which determine his goals. We can ask why Jones is mean or why he eats fish. The way it would be answered would depend on the context. It might be answered in terms of a rule-following type of explanation like 'because he is a Scotsman' or 'because he is a Roman Catholic'. This would assume some *established set of norms* and a system of training for handing them on. It would be radically different from the explanation 'because he is an anal character' or 'because he is an oral character'. For these explanations would presuppose that Jones was in some way a deviant from the norm of the circle in which he had been trained. It would state special conditions in his upbringing which occasioned his deviation. Whether or not such explanations, which presuppose fixation at certain periods of development, are causal or not, will have to be considered later.

Another way of answering the question 'Why does Jones eat fish?' would be to state in a tough-minded way 'because he likes it', or 'because it satisfies him'. This could be simply an impatient way of terminating the discussion or it could be an answer to the even more general question 'Why does a man eat anything?' At a common-sense level this is a very odd question; for 'a man must eat' is regarded as a decisive way of terminating a discussion. If pressed still further common-sense might reach rock-bottom with the truism that a man would die if he did not eat. The implication is the Hobbesian axiom that every man is afraid of death and that it makes no further sense to ask 'why?'

A variant on this type of answer is the assertion that a man needs food, which is very much like saying that a man *must* eat. For, at a common-sense level, the term 'need' is mainly normative. It prescribes one of a set of standard goals. It usually functions as a diagnostic term with remedial implications. It implies that something is wrong with a person if certain conditions are absent. We say things like 'The trouble with Jones is that he needs a wife' or 'Every child needs at least ten hours sleep.' The implication is that there is a state of affairs the absence of which is or is likely to be damaging to the individual in question. The individual, like a patient, may well be unaware of what this state of affairs is. Indeed, when we say that a person needs something, we are often indicating a discrepancy between what he actually does and what he ought to be doing. In other words the notion of 'need' in ordinary language is seldom *explanatory*. It is used to point out what a person ought to be doing rather than to explain what he is doing. It would only be an observer grossly over-sophisticated by Freudian theory who would say of a man leaping around in a Morris ring that old Jones obviously needs a woman, and who would think that he had *explained* his performance by pointing to the reality beneath the appearances. Reference to needs implies a standard pattern of prescribed goals; but it does not explain actions by reference to them. Whereas causal theories explain deviations from a norm, reference to needs prescribes the norms whose absence is thought to be injurious. It redirects attention to the accepted content of the rule-following purposive model.

Often we hear of 'basic needs' and 'need-reduction' in the context of explanatory theories in psychology. What has happened here is that conditions whose absence is thought to occasion injury have been interpreted in terms of a biological or physiological model. The answer to questions like 'Why does a man eat?' is provided by picturing an organism whose activities are directed towards survival or the preservation of equilibrium or some other such desirable and completely general end-state. This, of course, has to be broken down by giving an account of the particular conditions whose absence is thought to be injurious. Homeostasis, for instance, has to be described in terms of *particular* states like the temperature of the body and the level of blood-sugar. And, no doubt, postulating such conditions restored by various movements of the body in part explains them if the conditions restored are not part of what is meant by the description given to the movements. Sweating, for instance, may be a method of bringing about an optimum level of temperature in the body; but restoration of this level is not part of what is meant when we call certain movements 'sweating'. So saying that people sweat because it lowers the temperature of the body is explanatory.

But all too often this type of functional or end-state explanation is redescriptive rather than explanatory —especially when it is used for voluntary rather than for involuntary movements. This is when the conditions restored are part of what is meant by the activity to be explained. For instance it might be said that people dominate others because it reduces a need in them to do so. But what is the condition restored apart from that of the presence of others being dominated? What in this type of case is the equivalent of the temperature level which is restored by sweating? The homeo-static model of explanation is retained; but in the absence of specific states required to define what constitutes the equilibrium, it becomes entirely metaphysical. It is true that recourse is made to vague states of quiescence which the activity of dominating or acquiring money is alleged to bring about. But as there are no rules for identifying such states, their explanatory value is nil. Indeed in such cases need-reduction looks like a redescription of goal-seeking in terms which have the normative function of stressing the importance of conventionally prescribed pursuits. It is a justification masquerading as a high-level explanation.

Need-reduction explanations are a particular instance of a very common sort of explanation which will be termed 'explanations in terms of end-states'. For supervenient states of quiescence and satisfaction abound in psychological theories of motivation. It will probably be found that all such explanations share the logical features revealed in the specific case of need-reduction. These are (i) the generalization of a type of explanation that applies properly only to a very limited class of phenomena and (ii) the use of a term with highly general normative implications which obscure its emptiness as a highly general *explanation*.

The term 'end-state' has been chosen advisedly rather than the term 'end'. For one of the first things to be pointed out about these highly general sorts of explanation is that the ends postulated are not ends in the sense of 'end' or 'goal' employed in the purposive rule-following model. They are not—or should not be—postulated as answers to questions like 'Why did Jones walk across the road?' but as answers to questions like 'Why does a man eat?' or 'Why does a man smoke?'. They are therefore inappropriate as answers to lower order questions. For a man does not eat *in order to* reduce a need or relieve a tension. By eating, so the theories say, he in fact brings about such an end-state. Such explanations then do not give a man's reason for eating but the reason why he eats. But they differ from other cases of directed behaviour where we contrast *his* reason with *the* reason. For in other such cases—e.g. explanations in terms of unconscious wishes—we imply a goal *of the same sort* as that implied in *his* reason explanations, but we add the rider that the man does not envisage this goal as a conscious objective. We say, for instance, that *the* reason why he was unintentionally rude to his employer was because of his unconscious desire to injure a man like his father. But end-states are not goals like hurting a man, marrying a girl, or becoming Prime Minister. They are more mysterious states of quiescence, satisfaction, tension-reduction, and so on.

The theoretical interest of these types of explanation is that they are regarded as explaining *all* behaviour, whether of the rule-following sort or where there is a breakdown in behaviour and a cause is assigned, or when an activity—like dreaming—is of a sort such that it makes no sense to say 'What is the point of it?' Freud's pleasure principle is a good example; for he claimed

'In the theory of psycho-analysis we have no hesitation in assuming that the course taken by mental events is automatically regulated by the pleasure principle. We believe, that is to say, that the course of these events is invariably set in motion by an unpleasurable tension, and that it takes a direction such that its final outcome coincides with a lowering of that tension—that is with an avoidance of unpleasure or a production of pleasure.'

Some such homeostatic principle is so common in modern psychology that it has reached the standard text-books. To quote a typical case—Stagner and Karwoski (1952):

> 'The organism is endowed with an automatic equilibrium maintaining tendency which helps to preserve existence in the face of many kinds of environmental obstacles and difficulties.'

It is assumed that everything we do can somehow be subsumed under this very general principle. This assumption is so widespread and is so important to the claim that an over-all theory of motivation can be developed, that much more must be said about its appropriateness.

The assumption, to repeat, is that the reason why men eat, sleep, eliminate, and so on, is that achieving such goals relieves tension, restores equilibrium, produces satisfaction, and other such variations on a theme. This assumption is usually extended to cover all goal-directed behaviour—the pursuit of riches and foxes as well as the pursuit of water and women.

I will defer for a moment the problem of whether the postulation of such end-states is *ever* explanatory. For the issue is whether it *always* is. And this seems plainly false. For many goal-directed actions like posting letters, travelling to work, and passing the salt to one's neighbour do not seem invariably to be followed by such end-states. Indeed usually when we *say* that we get satisfaction or pleasure from doing something, we are not referring to some extra subsequent state of mind which we have become aware of by introspection. Rather we are saying two general sorts of things about it. In the first place we are saying that we were not bored, irritated, or distracted while we did it. We put our mind to the job in hand and concentrated on bringing about the required state of affairs. We were absorbed. The reference to satisfaction is not, in this case, an *explanation* of the pursuit of a goal, but a way of emphasizing that it really was a goal in the sense that our movements flowed towards it in an unimpeded and co-ordinated manner. Secondly the reference to satisfaction can be a way of stressing that the activity in question was done for its own sake and not as a means to something else. If a husband insists doggedly that he does the gardening because of the satisfaction he gets out of it he may simply be denying that he does it in order to help his wife with the housekeeping. He is not claiming necessarily that he glows and enters into a beatific state when the peas have been staked and the lawn cut. In other words, just as reference to need-reduction is a way of emphasizing the importance of some goals for the avoidance of injury, so reference to satisfaction is often a way of singling out others which are worth pursuing for their own sake. In a context of justification 'Because it satisfies him' is as final as 'Because he needs it'. What follows the 'because' are different facets of the bed-rock of justification. Psychologists have mistaken this bed-rock of justification for the apex of explanation.

Is it to be assumed, then, that reference to such end-states is *never* explanatory? All we have shown is that it is not *always* so. Clearly some such reference is reasonable in answering certain questions about the *body*, as was seen in the case of need-reduction.

Cannon, in his *Wisdom of the Body*, was indicating the evidence for bodily mechanisms of regulation and adjustment. The transition to using this type of explanation for voluntary actions rather than for the automatic adjustments of the body, comes about because it is suggested, e.g. by Freud—that types of stimulation brought about by departures from these optimum levels or end-states can only be mitigated by contact with the environment. The baby's hunger, for instance, is relieved only by contact with its mother's breast or with some equivalent source of supply. Its movements are at first random; but eventually, through the association of relief of tension with contact with the breast, a directed tendency develops which is activated by the stimulation of hunger. It is therefore concluded, probably erroneously, that whenever we find a case of such directed behaviour, it must be sandwiched in between tension and the reduction of tension. Yet even if such tension-reduction were an explanation of *acquiring* such a directed disposition, it would not follow that it also explained its *activation* later on after it had been acquired.

It is, however, significant that the sort of phenomena which have seemed to psychologists to require some sort of an end-state explanation, are those connected with learning and experimental types of situation. Thorndike's Law of Effect, for instance, postulated that successful responses were stamped in because of the satisfaction associated with contact with the correct goal. The pleasure-principle could well be vacuous as an all-embracing postulate, as envisaged by Freud; but it might well be part of the explanation of why certain directed sequences of

behaviour are *learnt*. And surely it would here coincide with the use of 'feeling of satisfaction' in ordinary
speech which cannot be analysed purely in the way
described above. For in exploratory and experimental
stages of an activity, before a habit has been formed,
or when we are confronted with obstacles that impede
habitual routines, we do speak of a feeling of satisfaction or a sense of achievement. If we are learning
to swim or to play golf or to walk after a long illness,
we do get a feeling of satisfaction or sense of achievement on attaining the goal. This is not exactly a
supervenient state extra to attaining the goal. The
feeling of satisfaction when one hits a good drive is
different from that attendant on hitting a good
niblick shot; and both are quite different from that
attendant on writing a good sentence or doing a good
dive. In the same way a hungry man gets satisfaction
from eating a beef-steak; but the type of satisfaction
is specific to the beef-steak. The end-states are not
exactly supervenient; rather they are descriptions of
the attainment of certain sorts of goals under certain
sorts of conditions. So in some cases which approxi-
mate in varying degrees to a learning, experimental
or obstacle type of situation, the postulated sequence
of tension, persistent and directed behaviour, and relief
of tension may well occur. But as most of our days are
spent in carrying out habits and routines, they do not
occur whenever there is a case of directed behaviour.
Indeed part of what we want to deny when we call a
piece of behaviour a habit is that it is a case of the varied, experimental, obstacle-ridden type of behaviour.

My point is therefore not that the reduction of
tension type of explanation is never relevant, but that

it explains the directedness of behaviour only under certain limited sorts of conditions. My objection to it is that it is so often used as an all-inclusive principle. For most psychological theories seem to accommodate their purposive or causal explanations under some such homeostatic postulate. The quasi-causal concept of drive, for instance, is usually subsumed under the general postulate of homeostasis; so is the purposive concept of the Freudian wish. But the relationship between these types of explanation and a homeostatic postulate is not of this deductive sort. It seems, to say the least of it, misleading to assimilate dreams and playing chess to shivering and sweating by maintaining that they are all particular cases of the maintenance of equilibrium—especially when the theorists, like Stagner and Karwoski, have to go on to distinguish static from dynamic homeostasis to make the suggestion even sound plausible! The quest for an all-inclusive explanation has led repeatedly to the obscuring of important differences by stressing trivial and highly speculative similarities.

Having distinguished the main sorts of explanatory questions that can be posed about human actions, the task is now to look at some typical psychological theories of motivation with the aim of discerning the types of questions which these theories are answering and of substantiating my claim that all-inclusive theories in this field are inappropriate. But it will be necessary, first, to say something about the concept of 'motive'; for this term has not been explicitly mentioned as a concept relevant to answering any of the types of questions distinguished. There are good reasons for this omission which must now be elaborated.

CHAPTER TWO

MOTIVES AND MOTIVATION [1]

'I am therefore going to commit a final and incorrigible lewdness. I am going to assess certain of the broad requirements for analyses of human motivation by examining human motivational phenomena.'   S. KOCH.

Introductory

THERE are two good reasons for dwelling on the use of the term 'motive' and 'motivation' before proceeding to a detailed analysis of psychological theories. In the first place, as I have argued elsewhere (Peters, 1956), the term 'motive' is used in specific sorts of contexts in ordinary language. The generalized use of this term by psychologists, some of whom hold that we have a motive for *everything* that we do, has therefore a rather bizarre effect, which it is the philosopher's task to make explicit.

Secondly the term 'motive' is <u>not</u> distinctive in that it does a quite different explanatory job from 'his reason' or 'the reason why'; rather it marks off certain sorts of reasons in certain types of contexts. Motives, in other words, are a particular class of reasons, which are distinguished by certain logical

---

[1] The main arguments of this chapter first appeared in an article bearing the same title in *Philosophy*, 31, (1956).

properties.   My thesis is that the concept of 'motivation' has developed from that of 'motive' by
attempting a causal interpretation of the logical force
of the term.   This is made possible by the failure
to distinguish different levels of questions.

I *The ordinary use of the term 'motive'*

Motives are a particular class of reasons. Many
sorts of things can be reasons for actions, but motives
are reasons of a particular sort. We can ask of a reason
for an action 'Was that his motive?'. But we cannot
ask of a motive, without in some way repeating ourselves 'Was that the reason why he did it?' Our preliminary problem about the concept of 'motive' is to
specify its delimiting criteria within the general class
of 'reasons for action'.

In certain contexts, instead of asking 'Why did
Jones do that?' we may ask what Jones' motive was.
Often this is in a context where it is appropriate to
ask 'What made Jones do that?'—when there is a
departure from the conventional expectations.   We
ask, for instance, what a man's motive is for com-
mitting a murder or for joining a party with whose
aims he is not in sympathy.   The implication is that
these actions are not characteristic of him or ones
which conform to any standard rule-following purposive pattern. But to ask for a man's motive is very
different from asking what made him do it in that it
strengthens rather than rules out the suggestion that
there was some point in what he did. When we say
'What made Jones cross the road?' we are most likely
implying that he had no objective in mind. We are

suggesting that something has happened to him rather than that he is aiming at something. But to ask for his motive is to suggest that this is very much a case of a directed action though the man's objective may be hidden from us as well as being pursued according to no standard pattern of rules.

There are, I would suggest, three characteristics shared by explanations in terms of motives which account for the difficulty in fitting them neatly into the framework of types of explanation which has been outlined. In the first place we only ask about a man's motives when we wish, in some way, to hold his conduct up for assessment. The word is used typically in moral or legal discourse where actions have to be *justified* and not simply explained. We ascribe or impute motives to others and avow them or confess to them in ourselves. This explains why we often ask for motives when there is a breach of conventional expectations; for it is in just these sorts of contexts that men have to justify their actions. It also explains the too easy connexion of the term 'motive' with early psycho-analytic explanations of the odd and unusual. Ordinary language can convey such subtle suggestions; for one way in which it differs from scientific language is that its use is not simply to describe and explain. It may command, condemn, guide, express states of mind, announce, provoke, exhort, and perform countless other such social functions. Often a different word is used precisely because such a specific social function is to be performed. Scientific language, almost by definition, has no such subtleties; and this is one of the difficulties which confront the theorist who uses a term like 'motive' in a special theory. The social implications of using the term haunt the theory.

This explains the sense of outrage which the ordinary man has when the psychologist gets busy on his motives. For psychologists tend to use the term indiscriminately and to ignore the contextual confinement of the use of the word in ordinary language. Some of them, indeed, suggest that we have a motive for *everything* that we do. The effect of such a suggestion is to put all actions up for assessment. We don't mind being asked our motive for effecting an entry into our neighbour's house without his permission; for this is the sort of action which obviously requires some sort of justification. But we take it amiss when our motives are questioned for getting married, playing chess, or giving Xmas presents to our friends. For in such cases we are doing the done thing and there should be no necessity for justification. Of course we probably have reasons for doing these sorts of things; people don't get married through force of habit or in a fit of absent-mindedness. But if we are asked about our motives the suggestion is that we may not have such obvious reasons. We may be up to no good. We may be marrying the girl for her money or giving Xmas presents to court popularity. When we are asked about our motives we may produce one that is a perfectly satisfactory justification, perhaps one that is usual in the circumstances. We might say, for instance, that we entered our neighbour's house to turn off the kettle which he had left boiling on the stove or that we were getting married in order to have a family. Similarly we can say that our neighbour is a man of the highest motives or that his motives in giving presents to his friends were unimpeachable. A motive is not necessarily a discreditable reason for acting, but it is a reason asked for in a context where there is a suggestion that it *might* be discreditable. The demand is for justification, not simply explanation.

From the point of view of ordinary usage it is bad enough for psychologists to suggest that we might have a motive for everything which we do. But matters become even worse when it is added that such motives may be unconscious. For the implication is that we may be up to no good and do not know it. This is a rather unnerving aspersion to have cast on our conduct. For the feeling of insecurity created by the suggestion that we may be at the mercy of unknown forces is aggravated by the implication that we may also be to blame for seemingly innocent acts. Fits of forgetfulness come to seem like intentional insults. And, in *some* respects they may be. But they are obviously not like them in that we could reasonably be said to be to *blame* for both. Yet the indiscriminate and extended use of the term 'motive' conveys just this suggestion. It has the unfortunate effect of blurring distinctions which are essential for practical life.

Motives, then, are reasons for action which are asked for when there is an issue of justification as well as of explanation. The question then arises as to the type of explanation that is offered when a motive is suggested. For not all reasons for action are motives. This is obvious enough; for we can ask whether a reason for an action is a motive. This brings us to the second characteristic of motives, that they are reasons of the directed sort. We may give a motive by alluding to a directive disposition like hunger, greed, or ambition. We say, for instance, 'His motive for marrying the girl was greed', or 'That politician's motive is ambition'. Or we can answer a question about a man's motive by quoting an exercise of such a directive disposition, as when we say 'He married her *for the sake* of her money', or 'he went into politics in *order to* advance himself'. All such explanations assign a goal to the individual whose motives are in question. Now, as I have shown, not all reasons for action are of this directed sort. We can explain a man's action in terms of traits of character, like considerateness, and punctuality. These may be reasons why people act; but they are not motives. For such terms do not indicate any definite sort of goals towards which a man's actions are directed. Motives, of course, may be mixed; but this only means that a man aims at a variety of goals by means of the same course of action. Similarly a man may have a strong motive or a weak one, an ulterior motive or an ostensible one. Such distinctions relate only to the influence of the goal on him or to the extent to which it is hidden. If he has a motive he must have a goal of some sort, however weak its influence or however obvious or attainable it may be.

It seems to me most important to insist on the directedness of motive explanations. For this aspect of motives has been sadly neglected in recent years both by philosophers and psychologists. The classic philosophical discussion of motives in recent years occurred in Ch. IV of Ryle's *Concept of Mind*. But, as I stressed on a previous occasion (Peters, 1952), Ryle's treatment of motives is very confusing because he uses the term 'motive' too much as a blanket term.

In his eagerness to refute the thesis that motives are mental occurrences—ghostly thrusts, to use his rather striking terminology—he claims that motive explanations always involve reference not to inner occurrences but to dispositions; but he groups together, quite indiscriminately, vanity, considerateness, patriotism, and interest in symbolic logic as examples of motives. Now these may well be dispositions, but they cannot all be appealed to as motives; for they do not all imply directedness. In rejecting the thesis that motives refer to inner emotional states, he fails to distinguish between the various types of disposition which he parades to take the place of the mythical emotional states. Psychologists, too, as I shall show later, have been guilty of a similar oversight. For in their interest in causes they have tended to equate motives with drives or initiating states of tension and have failed to stress the directedness of behaviour which is the cash value of assigning a motive to it.

This second characteristic of motive explanations links, to a certain extent, with features of the first. If we ask for a man's reason for doing something, the implication is that he is acting in no untoward way. His behaviour is within the framework of some rule-following purposeful pattern, but it is not clear which rule or which purpose it falls under. To ask for his motive, on the other hand, is only to ask for the end which explains his behaviour. The implication is that it is, to some extent, a departure from a habit or a purpose for the attainment of which there are conventions of appropriateness. We just want to know the goal which explains the sequence of his acts and the various moves he is making. The implication is that he is not sticking to standard moves. If we ask a man's motive for getting married we imply that this is, for him, merely an *efficient* way of getting to some end —e.g., the girl's money. It is not one of the standard or conventional ways of getting money. We are looking at what he is doing purely from the point of view of its being an efficient way of attaining an end. We cannot accept that the usual reasons for getting married fit his case. So we look around for some other reason that is operative.

This introduces naturally the third characteristic of motives as a class of reasons for action: they must be reasons why a person acts. By this is meant that the goal which is quoted to justify a man's action must also be such that reference to it actually explains what a man has done. The motive, in other words, must not be simply 'his reason'; indeed, in the case of 'unconscious motives' his motive cannot be *his* reason. The motive must be *the* reason why he did whatever he did. I have shown that we can also give *the* reason why a man acts in terms of non-directional dispositions (traits) or in terms of a *causal* theory. Motives are therefore only one particular type of answer to the question 'What was *the* reason why he did it?'. They involve the postulation of a type of goal towards which his behaviour was *actually* directed. We might, for instance, contrast the reasons which a man who is careless about his clothes gives for buying a new suit with his underlying motives. The implication of this contrast is that the objective which he pictures to himself or parades in public is not the one towards which his conduct is actually directed. This, it is implied, cannot be the reason why he bought the suit; it cannot therefore be his motive. But his reason might coincide with his motive. He might say that he bought the suit in order to impress his employer and this might also be the reason why he bought it. This would be an example of a conscious motive. If his motive was unconscious, then the reason why he bought the suit would be something like to attract the notice of his secretary, and the implication of saying that it was unconscious would be that he did not entertain this goal as a conscious objective. The intermediary case would be when his motive was equivalent to his *real* reason. In such a case he would put up a façade of impressing his employer but would not be deluding or deceiving himself about the actual reason for buying the suit. Of course he might have bought the suit both to impress his employer and to attract the attention of his secretary. If both reasons were in fact operative we would say that his motives in buying the suit were mixed. In other words, the distinction between conscious and unconscious, though important in some contexts, does not really affect the logical force of the term 'motive', which is to imply that, whatever he says or thinks about it, his behaviour is actually directed towards a certain type of goal.

My contention is therefore that there are three main characteristics of 'motive' as an explanatory concept in ordinary language:

(a) It is used in contexts where conduct is being assessed and not simply explained, where there is a breakdown in conventional expectations.
(b) It is used to refer to a reason of a directed sort and implies a directed disposition in the individual whose conduct is being assessed,

(c) It must state *the* reason why a person acts, a reason that is *operative* in the situation to be explained. The motive *may* coincide with *his* reason but it *must* be *the* reason why he acts.

Given this sort of analysis, further higher-order questions suggest themselves very easily. We might want to know, for instance, why certain types of reason are operative. Why are we inclined to accept sex, greed, ambition and hunger as motives, but would be incredulous if an anti-social man says that his motive for going to a party is to study his friend's furniture? Many would give the answer in terms of culture and knowledge of the individual in question. They would say that we only cite as motives those directed dispositions which are widespread, and dependable in a given culture. Indeed motives refer to those goals which exert so much influence on men that they will depart from their routines and flout social convention to attain them. To get on in the world is, in our culture, a widespread and insistent aim. Training and example exert a constant pressure on men to pursue this aim. Therefore if the evidence suggests that Jones is not lacking in ambition and if we can explain a piece of his behaviour in terms of his ambition, we are quite satisfied in claiming that ambition is his motive. But this would be but an elaboration of what could be called a structural theme —an indication of the structure of dependable goals in a given culture and of the organization of the character of the individual in relation to them. It would be of interest to anthropologists and sociologists, but of little interest to psychologists. For they would be looking for a different sort of answer to the question 'Why are such goals operative?'

The Oxford English dictionary, as a matter of fact, throws out hints about the sorts of things which have been of interest to psychologists. It defines 'motive' as

> 'That which "moves" or induces a person to act in a certain way; a desire, fear, or other emotion, or a consideration of reason, which influences or tends to influence a person's volition; also often applied to a contemplated result or object the desire of which tends to influence volition.'

This definition indicates well enough the directive aspect of the term 'motive'—the 'contemplated result or object' or the 'consideration of reason' which influences volition. But it also stresses the notion of 'moving' which is the etymological suggestion of the word, and its connexion with emotion and desire. And many would suggest that it is this connexion with emotion and movement which makes a reason a motive. It is an operative reason because of a causal connexion between directedness and some inner springs in the individual. A motive, it would be argued, is an emotively charged reason. The directedness of behaviour is set off by an emotional state. Motives, on this view, inhabit a hinterland between reasons and causes. They refer not only to the goal towards which behaviour is directed but also to emotional states which set it off.

Whether or not, in ordinary language, there is any such necessary connexion between giving the motive for an action and making any assertions of a causal kind about a man's emotional state before or when he does it, is difficult to say. My guess is that in general there is no such necessary connexion. Psychologists have developed quasi-causal theories to *explain* the directedness of behaviour, to answer the question 'Why are certain sorts of reasons operative?' and these theories may well have insinuated themselves into ordinary language as part of the meaning of "motive". It might well be, therefore, that people who are slightly sophisticated by psychological theories assume some such necessary connexion. But it would seem odd, when a question of motive is raised in a court of law, to ferret around for answers to questions about the emotions of the man whose conduct was being assessed. Evidence would be collected about what he was aiming at. But surely there would be little speculation about what *initiated* his purposeful behaviour.

II *The psychologist's concept of motivation*

Whatever the ordinary use of 'motive' may be in this respect, certainly it is the case that the concept of motivation, as employed by psychologists, entails more than the directedness of behaviour. It may well be that the meaning which they attach to this term illustrates the time-honoured psychologist's practice of giving a causal rendering of a logical point. The motive is the reason that is actually operative. This is a logical point—part of the analysis of what is meant by 'motive'. But the logical force of the term 'motive' has often been interpreted causally by postulating a particular sort of causal connexion between pursuing the goal and some inner spring of action. Bentham (1879 ed.), for instance, held that a motive was 'a pleasure, pain, or other event, that prompts to action', and there are many psychologists who followed him in postulating an antecedent state of emotion which initiates directed behaviour. Freud, too, regarded the 'wish' as an emotively charged idea, which acted as a kind of irritant, initiating behaviour. When, however, mentalistic interpretations fell out of fashion the notion of 'drive' became popular as a more tough-minded rendering of causal conditions which were thought to initiate goal-directed behaviour. Newcomb (1950) a fairly eclectic and representative American psychologist, makes this explicit when he says :

'Motive, like the non-technical terms "want" and "desire", is a word which points both inward and outward. Such terms refer both to an inner state of dissatisfaction (or unrest, or tension, or disequilibrium) and to something in the environment (like food, mother's presence, or the solution to a puzzle) which serves to remove the state of dissatisfaction.'

He says that an organism is motivated

'when—and only when—it is characterized both by a state of drive and by a direction of behaviour towards some goal which is selected in preference to all other possible goals. Motive, then, is a concept which joins together drive and goal.'

But what sort of a joining together is this? It looks like an analysis of the concept of 'motive' of a sort that implies that whenever we explain an action by reference to a motive we *both* assign a reason or goal *and* a cause. But are *both* elements of this ostensible analysis equally necessary? For it might be the case that when we have a motive we always have a goal but are only *sometimes* in some kind of an emotional state. Newcomb seems to accept this possibility implicitly when he later remarks rather charmingly :

'We do not have the means, for example, of distinguishing between the drive states of a given individual when he is motivated to win at poker and when he is motivated to win at tennis. The goals can easily be distinguished, but the drives cannot.'

Yet he can say that the individual who plays the two games is 'motivated' in spite of the fact that the causal component of the analysis—the drive state—cannot be identified. And rightly so—in spite of his analysis. For it is surely only the directedness of behaviour that is necessarily implied by saying that it is motivated.

Surely the reference to drives and emotions in relation to motivation is an attempt to answer questions *at a different level*. It is part and parcel of hedonistic and homeostatic theories which seek answers to questions like 'Why do men eat?' or 'Why do men eat at different rates?'. In other words reference to such causal conditions is an attempt to *explain* the directedness and persistence of behaviour. As 'motives' state goals towards which behaviour persists it is easy to see how particular theories *explaining* directedness have become incorporated in the *meaning* of 'motive'. Indeed this tendency has gone so far that the various Nebraska symposia on motivation have been mainly concerned with the operation of drives. The terms 'motive' and 'drive' have become almost synonymous. J. S. Brown (1953) for instance, in the first symposium suggested that

> 'one of the major sources of misunderstanding is the failure to distinguish clearly between drives or motives, on the one hand, and habits or reaction tendencies on the other.'

No one would dispute the importance of distinguishing explanations in terms of habits from other sorts of explanations ; but it is significant and typical of modern American thought that Brown should equate motives with drives in the course of separating off habits. Another typical example of this widespread tendency is Dollard and Miller. If we turn to 'Motivation' in the subject-index of their *Personality and Psychotherapy* we find two references. One of them is to a page where the typical sentence occurs : 'The attention of the therapist is forced on the drives that motivate behaviour.' There is then a significant bracket in the subject-index '(see also Drive)'!

Now perhaps a case can be made for some sort of drive theory as an answer to limited questions of the form 'Why does a man eat?' But, as I shall show later, this seems to be particularly obnoxious as an all-inclusive theory. Newcomb's embarrassment about the drive-state of a man who is motivated to win at poker as opposed to tennis is a typical consequence of an absurd theory. Even J. S. Brown (1953), a prominent drive-theorist, proclaims :

> 'We might advance more rapidly if we were to start afresh and deny at the outset that each and every object or situation for which an organism has learnt to strive must be accompanied by a characteristic drive for that object.'

D

This is a first step in the abandonment of drive-reduction as an over-all theory. But he should then also abandon any suggestion that there is a necessary connexion between having a drive and being motivated. For to strive for an object or situation is, at least under some conditions, to be motivated in respect of it; yet he wishes to deny that a man so motivated is necessarily driven towards it. Psychology's advance, at any rate towards conceptual clarity, would surely be more rapid still if it were admitted that it is only the directedness of behaviour that is entailed by saying that it is motivated, not any specific causal conditions, of 'drive' or anything else.

There are, of course, many like Hebb and McLelland who object strongly to the concept of drive but who wish to retain the concept of motivation. Yet, so it seems to me, they both make the same sort of conceptual mistake although they have different theories. Hebb (1949), for example, claims that

'The term motivation then refers (1) to the existence of an organized phase sequence, (2) to its direction or content, and (3) to its persistence in a given direction, or stability of content.'

He then goes on to say that his 'definition' means that motivation is not a distinctive process but is a reference in another context to the same process to which 'insight' refers. This, surely, is a terrible logical muddle. He rejects, for good reasons, the assumption of drive-theorists that directed and persistent behaviour is always preceded by various extra-neural bodily irritants postulated as antecedent causal conditions. In their place he postulates a central 'motive state', an organized phase sequence in the cells of the brain. He then proceeds to *define* motivation in terms not only of the directedness, organization and persistence of behaviour relative to a goal, but also in terms of this highly speculative condition of the brain. Now it might be the case that such a condition of the brain was *necessary* for the occurrence of motivated behaviour; but on his own showing it cannot be sufficient, since he claims that *all* voluntary behaviour, including 'insight', is also preceded by such a condition. But, leaving that difficulty aside, he surely cannot maintain that 'motivation' *means* a condition of the brain as well as the directedness, organization and persistence of behaviour. He, like everybody else, may be unsure on occasions what a man's motives may be ; but he, no more than anybody else, has to do a piece of physiological research in order to find out either what they are or whether he has any. He confuses the question of what we mean by 'motive' or 'motivation' with the question 'Why do men have motives?' or 'Why is behaviour organized, persistent, and directed relative to a goal?' The reference to phase sequences in the brain and to central motive states can only, surely, be a theory to *explain* motivation; it cannot be part of the *meaning* of motivation. And as a theory, it can at best, as I have suggested before, be only a statement of some of the necessary conditions of motivated behaviour. It cannot be a sufficient explanation of it. Physiological speculation is no substitute for empirical psychological research. Still less should it masquerade as part of the analysis of terms at a different logical level.

McClelland (1953), like Hebb, also launches some

devastating criticisms against various forms of drive theories. In their place he suggests an elaborate, ingenious, and often obscure hedonistic theory. 'A motive' he says 'is the redintegration by a cue of a change in an affective situation'. This is a very strange definition of 'motive'. For it surely confuses what is *meant* by 'motive' with a theory about how we come to have them. McClelland stresses that all motives are learned and learned in affective situations. This may be true. But it is surely irrelevant to the question of what is *meant* by 'motive.' His theory is that we are first of all presented with cues in affective situations; for instance, sugar is put in the mouth and this produces pleasurable affect. This type of cue then becomes paired with an affective state in such a way that the cue will, as a result of association, come to 'redintegrate' the affective state first associated with it. Behaviour gradually comes to be co-ordinated and directed towards situations which are associated with positive affect and away from situations associated with negative affect. Now all this story might be true. But even if it were, it does not follow that reference to redintegration should be included as part of the *definition* of 'motive'. One might as well say that all men pass through a stage of being a fish in the foetus and then go on to include a reference to this genetic fact in the definition of 'man'.

However, there is more to McClelland's view than a simple confusion between analysis and genetic speculation. He introduces his theory of genesis in the definition partly because he wants to insist on the necessary connexion between affect and motive. For him a goal must be a situation producing affect which is approached or avoided. He insists that 'only when succession of responses becomes a sequence which results in approach to or avoidance of a situation can we argue that there is evidence of a motive'. But there must be *affect* in connexion with the situation. Hunger, for instance, is based on two types of affective change—the innate pleasure from sucking and tasting, and the other based on reduction in internal stimulation arising from food deprivation. The motive of hunger, he says is

'to be defined in terms of adaptation levels in the mouth and stomach which can ordinarily only be changed by consequences of certain acts—chewing and swallowing food.'

A man with a motive of hunger has distinctive expectations and will engage in a varied course of actions which confirm these expectations in varying degrees and thus yield positive or negative affect.

Now there are two attractive features of this account of motivation. The first is that McClelland does resist the tendency prevalent amongst psychologists to say that *all* behaviour is motivated. The concept of motive is useful, he claims, only if it has some sort of limited base. He stresses that the essence of motivation is its capacity to elicit alternative behavioural manifestations. This would be one of the ways in which having a motive would differ from acting out of habit. For in our habits our actions are often directed towards goals, but they are stereotyped. This is part of what we mean by saying that an act is a case of a habit. And, as was brought out in treating the ordinary use of 'motive', we typically ask for a motive when behaviour seems to depart from an established routine. When we employ the concept of habit we are not denying that behaviour is directed; neither are we denying that it is in accordance with conventions. Indeed we are asserting that it *is* like this. But we are stressing the fixed nature of the pattern of behaviour of which it forms a part. When we ask for a motive, on the other hand, we are implying that the action is not habitual but that it is directed towards a goal. It is the goal that we are interested in. And anything is called a goal if we can see that behaviour *varies* concomitantly with changes in the situation which we call the goal and in the conditions necessary to attain it. Our problem is to fit the particular piece of behaviour into this rather fluid means-end nexus. In other words a man is either in some sort of experimental open sort of situation, where his routines are not fixed and we want to find his goal—a situation of such a sort that the sequence of his acts and the variations in his behaviour are made understandable as leading up to it; or he is under some extreme form of stimulation such that his routines are disrupted or telescoped, as when a starving man eats very quickly oblivious of his neighbours, or even takes the food up in his hands instead of using his knife and fork. If we ask for a man's reason for doing something we expect an answer in terms of the rule-following purposive pattern which is relevant to this sort of action. But when we ask for his motive we just want to know the goal towards which his behaviour is directed. The implication is usually that his behaviour is directed towards an end but that the means do not conform to any stereotyped, habitual pattern, or to any conventional canons of appropriateness. What he does is to be explained entirely by reference to the end which it seems to be directed towards. The only canons that are relevant are those of *efficiency* in relation to attaining the end. There is therefore much to be said for Allport's (1937) view that motives are 'habits-in-the-making'.

Granted, then, that it is the goal or a man's expectations of a goal that are up for scrutiny when we ask about his motives, what is to be made of McClelland's claim that this must always bring about a change in affect? He says, for instance, that the explanation 'the boy wants to do a good job' is a motive explanation because 'wanting to do a good job' defines an end situation which would produce positive affect. Does the reference to affect add anything to the claim that something is a goal? In my previous discussion of end-state explanations it was suggested that very often remarks like 'the boy wants a job' are synonymous with saying that he would be satisfied if he had a job, and that this would not state a prediction about his feelings when he got it but would be another way of saying that getting a job really functions as a goal for the boy—that his behaviour persists towards it and varies in accordance with changes in the situation defined as the goal. The question is therefore whether McClelland's insistence on affective arousal contains an additional empirical assertion to the effect that when a man has a motive he is always in an affective state, or whether his affective arousal theory is, in the main, a complicated analysis of what it means to have a goal which really is a goal. This can only be determined by a thorough examination of his account of affective arousal. But, at all events, his theory is more attractive than most in that he does de-limit the use of 'motive' in a way which is not unlike the ordinary use of the term.

The second attractive feature of McClelland's concept of 'motive' is that it is not a logically absurd view. As I have shown, there is a well-established tradition about the use of the word 'motive' which links it with emotion, which is made explicit by the Oxford English Dictionary. It is also a term in the same range of discourse. So to make reference to affect part of the meaning of 'motivation' would not be a logically preposterous suggestion like Hebb's attempt to include a reference to a phase sequence in the cell assemblies of the brain in the analysis of 'motive'. It would in fact be a return to the hedonistic tradition of Bentham and Mill. The question is, however, whether the reference to affect is part of the hedonistic answer to the question 'Why do men have motives?' rather than part of the analysis of 'motive'. Is McClelland's concept of 'motive' yet another example of explanation masquerading as analysis? This is obviously so in his definition which includes the reference to redintegration of affect. And it may be so in relation to his inclusion of any reference to affect in the definition of 'motive'. Decision on this point, however, will have to await a fuller considera-tion of his theory.

It might well be said that too much of this analysis has been made to hinge on the ordinary use of the term 'motive'. Why should psychological theories be fettered by the meaning attached to a term by non-specialists? After all, it might be argued, psychologists are not interested in assessing conduct when they speculate about motives. If they depart from the ordinary use of the term in this respect, why should they not depart from it in other respects?

There are two main answers to this objection. The first is to point out the dangers of using the same word in both a technical and a non-technical sense. A great deal of trouble, for instance, was caused in the 17th century by the technical meaning of the term 'body' in the new mechanical theories clashing with the non-technical meaning. (Peters, 1956). It is worth while dwelling on what may seem to be, at first sight, only a matter of terminology, because theories become popularised and the technical and practical implications of using the same term become confused.

The second answer is to stress that it is no accident that psychologists have lighted upon and developed the use of a term like 'motive' in their theories. For ordinary language enshrines all sorts of distinctions, the fine shades of which often elude the clumsiness of a highly general theory. The analysis of a concept like that of 'motive' is never merely an enquiry into terminology. It is an avenue of approach to distinctions which may well be theoretically as well as practically important. It has been argued, for instance, that the concept of 'motive' is needed to talk about the directedness of a man's behaviour in situations where he does not act out of habit and where he in some way seems to be departing from conventional expectations. He has a goal but does not seem to be following any set rule in attaining it, or he is indulging in some conventional piece of behaviour for reasons other than the obvious one. In practical life these are occasions when matters of assessment most frequently arise; hence the connexion between asking for the motive and asking for justification and not simply explanation. But from the point of view of explanation, the association of the concept of 'motive' with directedness and with behaviour that is not habitual or customary is most significant. For, whatever else psychological theories postulate, they usually make a reference to directedness part of their concept of 'motive' or 'motivation'. Theorists, too, as has been shown, are coming round to the view that it is misleading to say that *all* behaviour is motivated. Some make contrasts between 'drives' and habits; others between sequences of acts characterized by affective arousal and sequences that are affectively neutral. The point of looking closely at ordinary usage, if one is a psychologist, is that it often provides a clue to distinctions which it is theoretically important to take account of. We know *so much* about human beings, and our knowledge is incorporated implicitly in our language. Making it explicit could be a more fruitful preliminary to developing a theory than gaping at rats or grey geese.

Above all things, a study of the different psychological concepts of ordinary language encourages a sensitivity to the different *sorts* of questions that can be asked about human actions and the different sorts of answers that are appropriate. The specific sorts of questions connected with the concept of 'motive' have been distinguished and it has been suggested that over-all theories of motivation often create confusion by elevating an answer to a limited type of question to the status of a highly general postulate. To say, for instance, that all behaviour is motivated, is probably to announce from the start that crucial distinctions are going to be overlooked. However, this can only be shown by a more detailed look at the different theories. To this I shall now proceed.

CHAPTER THREE

FREUD'S THEORY

'Psycho-analysis grew on a narrowly restricted basis.'
S. FREUD

Introductory

A NEW YEAR is usually the occasion for signing a lot of cheques as well as for making
resolutions, and most of us have found ourselves
writing the date of the *previous* year in the top right
hand corner. At a conference a few years ago between
philosophers and psycho-analysts this sort of case
was dragged up and a long argument ensued as to
how it should be explained. The philosophers and
general psychologists favoured explanation in terms
of the persistence of a motor habit; the psycho-
analysts claimed that the mistake was due to our fear
of growing old and losing our virility. This is an
example of a borderline case where it is not absolutely
clear which sort of explanation is relevant, and where
they do not seem to be mutually incompatible. The
action might be 'overdetermined'. Many, of course,
would boggle at the intrusion of their loss of virility
into the matter; but they would concede that reference
to some kind of unconscious fear as well as to the
persistence of a habit might be relevant. If, on the
other hand, we get the date *right* on a cheque, reference

to an unconscious wish would be as out of place as would explanation in terms of the persistence of a habit, if, quite out of the blue, we put the date of the previous year in the middle of a year. In these cases the different types of explanation would exclude each other; for usually reference to unconscious wishes only seems relevant when explanations in terms of habit and conscious purpose break down.

This borderline case brings out the importance of approaching Freud's theory from the point of view of the sort of questions he was trying to answer as well as from the point of view of the types of answers that he gave. Freud's originality, as he himself indicated in his Introductory Lectures, was exhibited in his discoveries about unconscious mental processes, repression, and infantile sexuality. In these spheres, I shall argue, he was providing exciting answers to relatively limited questions. But he also tried to fit his speculations in these spheres into the framework of an ambitious over-all theory of a type that was neither plausible nor original—what he called 'the pleasure principle'. This theory derived from his early physiological research and added little to his psychological findings.

I *What did the theory of unconscious mental processes explain?*

It seems clear that Freud originally intended his theory of the unconscious to be used only to answer certain types of question in fairly specific contexts. What he says about this in his *Psychopathology of Everyday Life* (published in 1904) is worth quoting. He says that his explanations are relevant to 'Certain inadequacies of our psychic functions' and 'certain performances which are apparently unintentional'. The criteria for classifying them as such were :

(a) They must be faulty only 'within normal limits '— e.g., knocking a precious inkstand off the desk 'by mistake '.

(b) They must evince the character of momentary and temporary disturbance. The same actions must have been performed more correctly previously, or we must rely on ourselves to perform them more correctly. If corrected by others we must recognize the truth of the correction.

(c) If the action is perceived as faulty, the agent must be unaware of his motivation and explain it through 'inattention' or attribute it to an 'accident'. (Freud, 1914).

These rough and ready criteria make it clear that Freud thought his explanations relevant only to phenomena which can hardly be called actions in that they seem either to have no point or conscious objective or to fall short of standards of correctness. Examples would be forgetting a familiar name or knocking over a valuable possession while crossing a familiar room. On such occasions we should ask 'What made Jones do that?' and would accept some sort of causal explanation. The implication of Freud's criteria is surely that if a man exercises a skill correctly or performs a habitual routine, psycho-analytic explanation is out of place.[1] We might, of course, be

[1] Ernest Jones claims that in saying this I overlook "that such explanations do not apply merely to the faulty or neurotic situation, such as in everyday-life slips, but go far deeper to the ultimate origins of the action or interest ". But I am not denying that such research on "ultimate origins" might provide insight into certain *necessary conditions* of actions. All I am denying is that such research would supply a *sufficient explanation* of them.

unsure of the point of his performance or of the standard he was complying with. For instance, we might ask 'Why did Jones walk across the room? Was it in order to put coal on the fire or out of politeness?' But this would not be a causal question. It would be a way of eliciting what sort of action it was. Freud assumed a framework of correct and purposive behaviour and implied that reference to unconscious mental processes was only relevant when behaviour did not conform to such a framework.

As a matter of fact Freud often protested, as in 1922, that psycho-analysis 'has never dreamt of trying to explain everything'. As the science of the unconscious mind 'it has its own definite and restricted field of work' (Freud, 1950).[1] His claim was not that his theory could explain most human actions but that it could explain phenomena for which either no explanation had been forthcoming or only crude physiological explanations had been attempted. Lapses, at the common-sense level, are either regarded as inexplicable or assigned a crude bodily or physiological explanation like 'his hand slipped' or 'he was tired'. Freud's theory gave a *psychological* explanation of such phenomena and assigned them to a wider class of phenomena with which they had not previously been connected by theorists. In a paper called *The Claim of Psycho-analysis to Scientific Interest*, written in 1913, he spent a long time pointing out the relevance of his theories to general psychology.   He said :

'There are a large number of phenomena related to facial and other expressive movements and to speech, as well

[1] This is the date of the publication of the English edition, as always with dates in brackets in the case of Freud's works.

as many other processes of thought (both in normal and in sick people), which have hitherto escaped the notice of psychology because they have been regarded as no more than the results of organic disorder and of some abnormal failure in function of the mental apparatus. What I have in mind are "parapraxes" (slips of the tongue or pen, forgetfulness, etc.), haphazard actions and dreams in normal people, and convulsive attacks, deliria, visions and obsessive ideas or acts in neurotic subjects '. (Freud, 1955).

There is, from our point of view, a certainly significant family resemblance between these rather assorted phenomena. For it would be as inappropriate to ask for the point of a dream or a vision as it would be to ask for the point of a slip of the tongue or pen. We would naturally say 'What *made* me dream of a snake last night?' just as we would say 'What made my hand slip?' Similarly deliria, convulsive attacks, and visions are things that *happen* to people. We would not say 'What was the point of Joan of Arc's visions?' Rather we would say 'What caused them? Was it epilepsy?' They are all phenomena for which some kind of causal explanation seems appropriate. Obsessions, perhaps, are rather different; for they need explanation not because the acts involved have no point but because we cannot accept the point assigned to them. An obsessive may have a reason for what he does. In this way he is different from a dreamer or a man who forgets a name or whose hand slips. But, we cannot accept that his reason can also be the reason why he acts like this. A man who keeps on rubbing his hands in order to remove stains that manifestly are not there, or a man who keeps on returning to a room in order to see whether he has switched the fire off, would be examples. There is some-something odd or unconvincing about the reasons which they give for their acts; so we feel that some other sort of explanation is called for.

In the same article Freud mentioned only two other ways in which his theory was of interest to general psychology :

> ' Psycho-analysis ' he said ' unhesitatingly ascribes the primacy in mental life to affective processes, and it reveals an unexpected amount of affective disturbance and blinding of the intellect in normal no less than in sick people '.

Here again there is the suggestion of mental processes being disrupted, of failing to come up to standards. Psycho-analysis explains such deviations; but it does not explain cases where the intellect is not blinded.

The question then arises whether explanations in terms of unconscious wishes are appropriate *only* to cases where there is some sort of a lapse or break-down and to cases like dreaming and hallucinations where it is inappropriate to ask what the point of the performance might be. What of those influenced by psycho-analysis who suggest that there is an un-conscious motive for *everything* that we do? The plausibility of this suggestion derives surely from cases where people give *unconvincing* reasons for what they do and where psycho-analysis provides a con-vincing explanation. For instance, if a schoolmaster administers corporal punishment very readily on the grounds that it is beneficial to the boys, we are

E

inclined to accept the explanation that he does this out
of repressed sadism rather than out of concern for the
boys, simply because the conscious reason is not a
very convincing one. For what is the evidence that
in most cases corporal punishment has the results
that are claimed for it? But there are cases when we
would be perfectly agreeable to say that *both* conscious reasons and unconscious motives were relevant.
For instance a doctor might decide to operate very
quickly on an abscess on the grounds that it was
essential to stop the poison spreading in the patient's
system; this would be a perfectly satisfactory conscious reason. Yet he might also be acting out of
unconscious sadism, as well as out of concern for the
patient. Freudians sometimes impute repressed sadism
to other psychiatrists who use electric shock treatment. But we would only accept their explanation as
sufficient if there was little evidence to suggest that in
fact electric shock treatment has beneficial effects on
those who are subjected to it. If the stated reason for
an action is not unplausible as an explanation of it,
we might say that the action was 'over-determined';
but it would be odd to discount the conscious reason
because there was *also* a plausible explanation in
terms of an unconscious wish. After all people have
mixed motives at the conscious level for doing things.
A man might give a bed to a hospital out of his
desire for social approval as well as out of his concern
for suffering. And he might be well aware of both
reasons for giving the bed. A surgeon, too, might use
the knife both out of concern for suffering and out of
sadism; but the fact that the latter motive might be
unconscious matters little. Plurality of causes is

common enough in the natural world. There is no reason to suppose that actions must have only one motive. In cases where an explanation in terms of conscious reasons is sufficient—e.g., taking a bishop in order to checkmate the king—there are obviously also causes of the action like movements in the muscles and central nervous system. The point is, however, that if it is an action it is not *sufficiently* explained in terms of such causes.

This gives the clue to the sort of trouble that can arise in the case of unconscious motives; for they are often regarded as *sufficient* to explain what purports to be an action, rather than a lapse from an action. The conscious reasons, which make it look like an action, are regarded as being in some way irrelevant or illusory, an excuse for what the man is going to do anyway. Some such theory, as a matter of fact, was advanced by Freudians, who held that *some* reasons for actions are rationalizations,[1] a façade that we erect so that we can satisfy dangerous wishes in a manner that is socially acceptable. But, surely, we are led to say that something is a rationalization *because the reasons are suspect anyway*, because they fail to satisfy certain obvious common-sense standards. If, for instance, the schoolmaster still persists in administering corporal punishment as a panacea for childhood-aberrations in the absence of evidence one way or the other, or after being confronted with a lot of evidence

[1] Ernest Jones has pointed out to me that Freud himself did not use the concept of 'rationalization'. Indeed, as far as I know, Jones himself was the first to use it in his paper on *Rationalization in Everyday Life* which he read at the First International Psycho-analytic Congress in 1908. Freud used a similar sort of concept—that of "idealization".

showing that its effects were quite otherwise than he thought, we would only then begin to say that his reasons were rationalizations. But this would be because considerations which were logically relevant to his belief about the efficiency of corporal punishment in bringing about an avowed end in no way affected his pursuit of the end. His case would be like that of an obsessive who gives a reason for what he does, but what he does seems peculiarly ill-adapted to bringing about the end for the sake of which he says that he does it. But it would be logically absurd to say that *all* reasons were rationalizations; for this would make the distinction between the two non-sensical. It is only because people sometimes give genuine reasons for what they do, and because they sometimes change their course of action in the light of considerations that are logically relevant to the end that they have in mind, that it makes sense to talk of rationalizations as distinct from reasons. The term 'rationalization' is a parasite. It flourishes because common experience has provided hosts in the form of genuine reasons for action.

Surely, too, there are a great number of cases—e.g., walking on the side of the on-coming traffic, where there is no footpath—which have such an obvious and acceptable explanation in terms of conscious reasons that it seems absurd to look around for unconscious motives. This, I think, Freud would have been perfectly prepared to accept; for, though he held that much of the ego was unconscious, he thought that the ego-instincts, concerned with self-preservation, were more influenced by the reality principle and less subject to repression than the sex instincts. In such cases the conscious reasons are obviously sufficient to explain what a man does; *his* reason coincides with *the* reason why he acts.

My conclusion, then, is that there is a kind of gradation in the relevance of explanations in terms of unconscious wishes. Some actions have such obvious and acceptable reasons that reference to unconscious wishes seems grotesquely out of place. There are then actions, like that of the surgeon, where good explanations in terms of conscious reasons can be supplemented either by other motives or by postulating unconscious wishes as well. These are 'overdetermined' actions. Then there are actions where the stated reason is *unconvincing*. In such cases the first move is usually to look round for a *concealed* conscious motive. It is sometimes said that Henry VIII contracted many marriages in order to obtain a legitimate heir. But even if he had said this he might well have been aware that he really desired something else. We look first, in such cases, for a man's *real* reason, of which he may well be conscious, but which he keeps to himself or to his bosom companions. But often there is no such concealed reason; and in such cases we have recourse to unconscious wishes which are *sufficient* to explain what he does. But it is only when the stated reasons are unconvincing as explanations that we look round for unconscious wishes as *sufficient* explanations. It looks, therefore, as if recourse to unconscious wishes is appropriate in cases where there is something palpably inefficient about an act in relation to the point ascribed to it as well as when an act seems to have no point.

II *What types of explanation did Freud employ in his theory of the unconscious?*

So much for the sort of phenomena which Freud's theory of unconscious mental processes was designed to explain. The question to be considered now is the sort of explanation that he offered. Much has been made in recent discussions of the thesis that Freud's theory of unconscious wishes is a way of offering reasons for phenomena which were previously thought to be explicable only in terms of causes. It is often asserted, even, that Freud showed that men are more rational than was previously assumed, that he extended the model of a man adopting means to ends into the unconscious. Now this is an attractive and exciting thesis and one that appeals to those who believe in the rationality of man. But it is riddled with ambiguities, and, in escaping the pushes and pulls of causal explanation, it overlooks crucial logical distinctions implicit in the use of various different concepts and fails to do justice to what many would claim to be Freud's most distinctive teaching about unconscious mental processes.

To start with the logical distinctions which are important in this context: Freud's theory was one of unconscious *wishes*, not of unconscious reasons. The importance of this distinction can be shown by an example. Suppose that Jones is unintentionally rude to his employer while trying to be nice to him. The Freudian explanation might be that the employer stood for his father and that he unconsciously wished to hurt him. Now this would not be *Jones'* reason for being rude. For, as we have shown, the concept of 'his reason' implies consciousness of an objective and envisaging the steps necessary to attain it. It would be a contradiction in terms to say that *his* reason for being rude was to hurt his employer but that he did not envisage hurting him. Of course his unconscious wish to hurt his employer could be *the* reason for being rude to his employer. But, as I have shown, so could a lot of other things. *The* reason, for instance, might be a causal explanation like 'his nerves were on edge'; or it might be a trait like 'tactlessness'; or it might be a directed disposition like 'aggressiveness'. The concept of 'wish' is very like the concept of 'motive' in that it always emphasises directedness. But it is unlike the concept of 'his reason' in that it implies no grasp of the means necessary to attain what is wished for. Whereas the concept of 'motive' implies an end and a sequence of acts that are *efficient* (though perhaps not socially appropriate) for bringing it about, the concept of 'wish' does not even imply efficient means. Indeed we usually refer to people's wishes when we want to speak of ends without any implication about their practicality. It could be said that Freud's theory involves the extension of the concept of 'wish' in that we usually imply that a person *consciously* entertains an end when we speak of his wishes. But this is not to say that he extended the concept of 'his reason' also which implies that a man envisages both an end and means that are both efficient and socially appropriate for attaining it.

As a matter of fact, to argue for an extension of the concept of 'his reason' to the unconscious involves the abandonment of what many would regard as Freud's distinctive contribution to our understanding of the unconscious. For, to quote Ernest Jones :

> '. . . Careful students have perceived that Freud's revolutionary contribution to psychology was not so much his demonstrating the existence of an unconscious, and perhaps not even his exploration of its content, as his proposition that there are two fundamentally different kinds of mental processes, which he termed primary and secondary respectively, together with his description of them. The laws applicable to the two groups are so widely different that any description of the earlier one must call up a picture of the more bizarre types of insanity. There reigns in it a quite uninhibited flow towards the imaginary fulfilment of the wish that stirs it—the only thing that can. It is unchecked by any logical contradiction, any causal associations; it has no sense of either time or of external reality. Its goal is either to discharge the excitation through any motor exit, or, if that fails, to establish a perceptual,—if necessary, an hallucinatory— identity with the remembered perception of a previous satisfaction' (Jones, 1954).

This surely amounts to saying that in so far as unconscious processes are involved, the thinking about getting to the goal cannot be described as either correct or incorrect, efficient or inefficient, intelligent or unintelligent. It just happens according to mechanical principles. The point is not simply that the logic of the term 'wish', whether conscious or unconscious, is different from that of 'his reason' in that the latter implies criteria of efficiency, correctness, and so on, in reaching an objective. It is also that Freud's description of unconscious processes denies explicitly the relevance of such criteria in cases where an unconscious wish is postulated to explain an action or a process of thought. At the conscious level a wish becomes a reason for acting when logical and causal connexions, together with norms of social correctness, are grasped to connect what is wished for—the objective—with acts that lead on to it. But in the case of unconscious processes the connexion is not one of logical or causal relevance. It is one that Freud describes in causal terms transferred from a physio-logical theory. For, in his early days at any rate, Freud peered at a patient in the manner in which he had peered at nerve-fibres through a microscope, and thought of a human being to a certain extent, as an enlarged and more complex structure obeying the same sort of laws and working by means of the same sort of mechanisms as the cells and neurones com-prising the body.

Freud's physiological speculations dated back to the 1890's, when, during the period of his strange association with Fliess, he composed in rather a feverish and compulsive manner his *Project for a Scientific Psychology*. He very soon regretted his sortie into speculation and refused to allow the *Project* to be published; but in spite of his overt rejection of his theorizing, the leading ideas of his Project appear repeatedly in his later works. He never abandoned Hobbes' hoary hypothesis, developed in detail in the *Project*, that psychical states were reflections of material elements subject to the laws of motion. The material elements in question were conceived of as neurones, the theory of which he took over from his neuro-histological studies. 'Nervous excitation' was regarded quantitatively and thought of as subject to the principle of inertia, which stated that neurones tend to get rid of excitation. Reflex movement, where sensory excitation is followed by motor discharge, would be an example. Paths of discharge develop for ending stimulation. But there are some stimuli— internal ones—which cannot be got rid of by simple paths of discharge or by flight. So help has to be obtained by bringing about specific changes in the outside world—e.g., by eating food. So eating is a method of abolishing an internal stimulation. These basic assumptions re-appear in his famous paper in 1915 on *Instincts and their Vicissitudes* where he still held that the main function of the nervous system was to abolish stimuli or to reduce excitation to the lowest possible level. Instincts, he held, are stimuli to the mind arising from an internal source—e.g., the parched membrane of the oesophagus in the case of thirst (Freud, 1925). Flight is of no avail against such a stimulus; so a suitable alteration in the inner source of stimulation will have to be brought about if the stimulus is to be abolished.

His account of the mind simply mirrored this physiological description. Mental energy takes the place of the physiological notion of the quantity of excitation; mental contents, such as ideas, take the place of neurones, and the postulate of inertia—that neurones tend to get rid of excitation—is replaced by that of pleasure-unpleasure which reflects, in the mind, the mastering of stimuli. The wish is a current in the mind that arises from unpleasure and ends in pleasure, achieved by the discharge of tension through the motor apparatus. If movements do not alter the source of stimulation unpleasure persists, though temporary satisfaction may be obtained by activating a memory trace of a previous perception associated with satisfaction. When the current activates such a memory, Freud calls it 'hallucinatory wish-fulfilment' —common in dreams and in the psychoses. In the pure pleasure-principle wishes persist until either a memory trace associated with previous decrease of excitation is activated, or some motor activity takes place which relieves the initiating tension. But in these *primary* processes of thought, under the dominance of the pure pleasure-principle, there is no orderly progression from tension to motor activity which has been found by experience to relieve the tension. This can only come about when *secondary* processes of thought, employing the reality principle and proceeding in accordance with logical rules and canons of causal inference, develop. In the realm of the pure pleasure-principle thought proceeds only according to mechanical principles. There is, for instance, the principle of *emotional equivalence* based on the association of ideas with a discharge of tension. These ideas can be *displaced* so that the object associated with the discharge of one type of instinctive excitation can serve as the object of another. Similarly an object like a snake can appear instead of another like a penis because it is emotionally equivalent. The logical relation of representing, which characterises symbols of conscious thought, is not employed. Such processes are regulated entirely by the tendency towards discharge of tension—i.e. pleasure—and there· is no discrimination in terms of efficient and inefficient, correct and incorrect, real and imaginary. Like the movements inside a battery, they just happen.

So, to revert to my example, if a man is unintentionally rude to his employer, the explanation might be that the sight or thought of a man who was emotionally equivalent to the father initiated tension which must persist until some kind of discharge is found. The discharge might take a hallucinatory form in dreams. The man might dream of killing his employer or some similar father-figure; or it might be discharged through the motor apparatus by his being rude or treading on his toe 'by mistake'. The explanation is of a causal type; he is, as it were, pushed into being rude by the wish or current seeking some form of discharge. The manner of discharge is explained in terms of past associations. It is surely a parallel to the kind of explanation that would be given of a man being stung by a wasp while driving a car. His driving would be disrupted by his leap in the air which would be a motor response to this sort of stimulus established by past conditioning. It would be, to use Freud's phrase, a 'flight from stimulation'. We would ask what *made* him leap in the air. The implication would be that he had no reason for it; it was caused. Freud transfers this itch-scratch picture of stimulation and response to the mind which is regarded as a mechanical system.

The model of explanation is very different, however, when Freud talks of secondary processes, of the Ego as opposed to the Id, and of the Reality principle as opposed to the pure pleasure principle. At this level the nicely calculated more or less takes the place of impulsive plunges. 'The ego represents what we call reason and sanity, in contrast to the id which contains the passions'. (Freud, 1927). The Ego, he says, arranges the process of the mind in a temporal order and tests correspondence with reality, it interposes a process of thinking and controls the avenues to motility; it holds a position in the mind like that of a constitutional monarch, striving to bring the id into subjection and defending itself against the demands of the super-ego. Now this is very figurative sort of talk. Freud, surely, is here indulging in the familiar practice of constructing a model of the mind to make logical distinctions between different types of explanation. When Freud wants to describe goings-on of which it is appropriate to say that a man is acting, that he has a *reason* for what he does, and so on, he talks about the Ego; when on the other hand, he wants to say that a persons suffers something, or is made or driven to do something, he speaks of the Id. The concept of the Ego makes explicit the sorts of things that are pre-supposed in having a reason for acting. It 'tests correspondence with reality'; it 'interposes a process of thinking'; it 'secures postponement of motor dis-charges'; it 'subjects the id' and 'defends itself against the super-ego'. These verbs are only used appropriately of *persons*, not of hypothetical parts of the mind. By speaking of the Ego as a sort of agent in the mind Freud was not *explaining* human actions; he was merely making explicit what they are as distinct from, and in relation to, various forms of passivity. Just as Locke invented 'simple ideas' to make logical points about the evidence for certain sorts of statements, so Freud used the model of the Ego and the Id to bring out that sometimes we take account of facts, act deliberately, plan means to ends, and impose rules of prudence on our conduct, whereas at other times we take no account of facts, act impulsively, and are driven, obsessed and possessed.

Freud, of course, made the extremely fertile and useful suggestion that acts can be unconsciously as well as consciously *directed*. But his stress on the different characteristics of the primary and secondary processes of thought implied that if a man's doings are to be explained in terms of an unconscious wish he is behaving more like a moth veering towards a light than a helmsman steering a ship to port.   In his later years he may well have become increasingly sceptical about the quasi-physiological speculations of his youth. For instance, in his last work in 1940, *An Outline of Psycho-analysis*, he stressed the mysteriousness of unconscious processes 'For here we have approached the still shrouded secret of what is mental.' (Freud, 1949). But he did suggest that we have, in this sphere, a theory of energy which exists in two forms 'one freely mobile and the other, by contrast, bound; we speak of cathexes and hypercathexes of the material of the mind' . . . He then went on to say :

'But behind all these uncertainties there lies one new fact, the discovery of which we owe to psycho-analytic research. We have learnt that processes in the unconscious or in the id obey different laws from those in the preconscious ego. We name these laws in their totality the *primary process,* in contrast to the *secondary process*. which regulates events in the preconscious or ego'.

He also, in his next chapter on dreams, stressed the illogicality of the unconscious which 'might be called the kingdom of the illogical'. The Id, he said, 'sets

more store by the opportunity of discharging quant-
ities of excitation than it does by any other consideration'. So it seems fairly safe to say that right
up to the last Freud insisted on the radical difference
between explanations in terms of conscious and unconscious processes and that he retained his causal 'excitation' model for his theory of psychic energy in the Id.

III *The pleasure-principle as an over-all postulate*

So far I have claimed that Freud had *two* theories
—one to explain actions and the other to explain
lapses from action, inefficient action, and phenomena
which fall outside the category of action. But it
might be argued that he unified these two theories by
means of an all-inclusive theory—his pleasure
principle. He probably thought of it as a unified
theory; for it was a relic of his early physiological
speculations in the *Project*—where he made con-
jectures about the underlying material basis of
Ego-functions as well as of dreams, hallucinations, and
other psychotic states. But, if the details of his
pleasure principle are studied, it will appear that it
breaks down into two principles and that, as an over-
all postulate, it is inadequate because of the very
limited range of phenomena which it in fact explained.

(*a*) THE THEORY STATED. Freud seemed to think
that, although conscious acts could not be sufficiently
explained in terms of unconscious processes any more
than slips, lapses, dreams, phantasy, etc., could be
explained in terms of conscious processes, nevertheless both conscious and unconscious processes were

explicable in terms of the general tendency to seek pleasure or avoid pain. For he said :

> 'In the theory of psychoanalysis we have no hesitation in assuming that the course taken by mental events is automatically regulated by the pleasure principle. We believe, that is to say, that the course of those events is invariably set in motion by an unpleasurable tension, and that it takes a direction such that its final outcome coincides with a lowering of that tension—that is, with an avoidance of unpleasure or a production of pleasure (Freud, 1925).

In his *Beyond the Pleasure Principle* he linked this principle with Fechner's hypothesis that—

> 'every psycho-physical movement crossing the threshold of consciousness is attended by pleasure in proportion as, beyond a certain limit, it approximates to complete stability, and is attended by unpleasure in proportion as, beyond a certain limit, it deviates from complete stability' (Freud, 1922).

Freud held that unpleasure and pleasure reflect the manner in which the process of mastering stimuli takes place, pleasure reflecting merely the abatement of stimulation. In the case of hunger and thirst he spoke of 'needs' which spring from stimuli of instinctual origin like hunger contractions and the parched state of the oesophagus. Every instinct has such a source—a somatic process from which the stimulus results; an aim—the satisfaction obtained by abolishing the source of stimulation; and an object —that in or through which the aim is achieved (Freud, 1925). The object, Freud thought, is the most variable thing about an instinct and becomes attached to it only in consequence of being peculiarly fitted to obtain satisfaction. In other words Freud explained the attachment (cathexis) to and pursuit of various objects by the role which such objects played in the reduction of stimulation. For instance attachment to the breast developed because of its initial efficacy in reducing the stimulation of hunger and its later association with 'organ-pleasure' in the region of the mouth associated with sucking.

(b) CRITIQUE OF THE THEORY.

(1) *Two principles not one.* Enough has already been said in relation to the Ego and the Id to show that, although Freud spoke generally of the pleasure-principle, he insisted that there were in fact *two* principles of mental functioning. Indeed in 1911 he wrote a paper with this very title. To quote Ernest Jones (1955):

'The two principles Freud here established, which he termed the "pleasure-principle" and the "reality-principle" respectively, are really extensions of the distinction he had pointed out fifteen years before between the "primary system" and the "secondary system" of mental functioning. It was this distinction on which rests Freud's chief claim to fame: even his discovery of the unconscious is subordinate to it'.

Freud claimed that the reality principle safeguarded but did not dethrone the pure-pleasure principle. The latter can do nothing but wish and work towards the gaining of pleasure and the avoiding of pain; but the former strives for what is useful and guards the Ego against damage. Uncertain, momentary pleasure is given up to gain an assured pleasure later. But the Ego, employing the reality principle, only gradually gains the ascendancy. The sexual instincts are particularly difficult to bring under conscious control, and part of mental life, in phantasy and dreams, remains under the sway of the pure-pleasure principle. Hence the close connexion between sex and phantasy. This dichotomy of Freud's presents in a genetic and pictorial form, the difference, which has been laboured, between a man acting deliberately and purposefully and being subject to various states which do not come into the category of 'actions'. Yet it might be argued that these are still only two ways in which the fundamental transition from un-pleasure to pleasure takes place. It might well happen at both the conscious and unconscious level and be governed by the different laws that regulate happenings at these levels; but it still always happens.

(2) *Is the principle universally applicable?* Some such principle may *sometimes* operate in the process of learning motives and after they have been learnt. But the question is whether it *always* does—which seems improbable. It has been shown, for example, that animals will go through the motions of eating and drinking without stomachs and with their throats anaesthetized. Also eating and drinking stops *before* the relevant nutrient can be absorbed sufficiently to produce a marked change in internal stimulation. Furthermore the experiments of Olds and others show that, if an electrode is placed in parts of the hypothalamus and mid-brain, animals will persistently seek stimulation and will prefer this sort of self-stimulation, even when hungry or thirsty, to consuming

food or water which classically were regarded as methods of 'mastering' stimulation from other parts of the body (Olds, 1955). In the face of this kind of evidence it is difficult to maintain that all actions and processes of thought are methods of transition from stimulation to its abatement. And these are the most favourable sorts of cases where there is a *prima facie* case for a terminating state of 'satisfaction'; for in most cases of directed behaviour, as Tolman (1932) was honest enough to admit when he distinguished first-order from second-order drives, there are no such recognizable physiological concomitants of states of 'satisfaction'. Freud (1925), it is true, said that the study of the sources of instincts lay outside the scope of psychology. 'We do not know whether this process is regularly of a chemical nature or whether it may also correspond with the release of other, e.g., mechanical, forces' (p. 66). He claimed that in mental life we know instincts by their aims. But, surely, such 'aims' or terminating states of 'satisfaction' are as elusive and nebulus as the alleged stimulation which is being abolished.

It is, of course, no doubt true that the model of explanation presented by Freud *sometimes* has application. There are *some* occasions when stimulation occurs which is painful and when behaviour persists until the stimulation abates. Sitting on an ant-hill or a thistle, extreme hunger, and urination when the bladder is very full seem obvious examples. Talk of tensions, discomfort, pain, and the removal of such conditions, seems obviously to fit such cases and to explain the directed actions which are usually fitted into this particular form of the hedonistic sandwich.

It is quite probable, too, that this sort of model describes very well some sorts of conditions under which *some* directed sequences are learnt. But it is unplausible to suggest even that all cases of eating and urination can be fitted into such an explanatory formula, let alone other cases of directed behaviour like playing chess, going to meet a friend, or making a bed, where the model seems quite out of place. Of course discomfort and so on may well be generated if habits are disrupted or if we are frustrated in the pursuit of a goal. But this does not imply that any sort of discomfort initiates directed behaviour when all is going smoothly.

(3) *Exclusively an avoidance theory.* The implausibility of suggesting that Freud's over-all postulate applies universally is in part due to its being exclusively an *avoidance* theory. The man who climbs Everest in the face of the most severe forms of discomfort must somehow be escaping from discomfort which initiates his activity. If doubt is cast on the hypothesis because the climber denies that he felt any such discomfort before deciding to embark on the climb, there are two possible moves open to the Freudian. He can claim that there is tension in the mental system which does not emerge as discomfort in consciousness; or he can have recourse to Freud's later theory and maintain that some acts are not flights from existing discomfort but the avoidance of anticipated discomfort. For in his later work on *Inhibitions, Symptoms and Anxiety*, Freud suggested that anxiety was a *signal* of the approach of a danger situation occasioned by the arousal of a threatening wish in the unconscious which the Ego anticipated

and prepared itself against, rather than, as on the earlier theory, the felt aspect of a danger situation.

Whatever move, however, the Freudian makes to deal with such obvious counter examples, he is committed to defending a very unplausible form of hedonism. For, on Freud's theory, pleasure is nothing positive. It denotes varying degrees of the abatement of pain, and this in its turn is linked with the theory that stimulation occasions pain. Freud, it is true, did say (Freud, 1922) that there was no simple relation between the strength of feeling and the quantity of excitation. But he definitely thought that unpleasure was the mental manifestation of stimulation. Yet many forms of stimulation are pleasant rather than unpleasant. It is probable that whether stimulation is painful or not depends, as McClelland suggests, on the amount of the discrepancy between expectation and actual occurrence rather than on stimulation *per se*. Also many activities like thinking, gardening and talking to friends may be pleasant in themselves; it is odd to look on them as ways of getting rid of pain. This distinction between 'pure' and 'impure' pleasures goes back to Plato and Aristotle; it is salutary to see a renewed interest in its importance amongst modern psychologists, which will be discussed in the last chapter of this monograph.

The root of the inadequacy of Freud's theory was probably his physiological orientation. He held an antiquated theory of the nervous system which maintained that activity is always occasioned by stimulation, whereas nowadays it is held that the nervous system is in a constant state of activity and explanation is needed of the patterning of activity rather than of its initiation. His next step was to assume that all stimulation is painful. The logic of the concept of 'pain' or 'unpleasure' together with a lot of supporting cases in ordinary experience did the rest. For 'pain', almost by definition, is something that has to be got rid of, there being many examples of directed sequences of behaviour which obviously get rid of pain. So given the hypothesis that all activity is the product of stimulation, together with the assumption that stimulation is always unpleasant, the over-all theory follows necessarily. But, like many such over-all theories, it depends upon following the logic of a concept which fits some cases and applying it rigorously and ingeniously to all cases. This was made more plausible, as has been shown, by the translation of physiological concepts into psychological terms, at any rate in respect of the primary processes, the realm under the sway of the pure pleasure-principle. A crucial example of such a translation is the assumption that the transition from unpleasure to pleasure is the mental equivalent of the transition from stimulation to its abatement. By this sort of logical leger-de-main a mistaken physiological theory was perpetuated as an all-embracing psychological postulate.

IV *Infantile Sexuality and the Mechanisms of Defence*

So far I have considered the types of question answered by Freud's theory of unconscious mental processes and the type of explanation involved. I have also considered the pleasure principle as an example of an over-all postulate purporting to explain both conscious and unconscious processes of thought. Freud, however, gave much more specific explanations of the directedness of behaviour than this. Whereas his pleasure principle was merely an attempt to fit his psychological theory into a traditional mechanical model, his speculations about infantile sexuality and the mechanisms of defence were highly original and relatively independent of such a model. Indeed one of the puzzles about these explanations is to be clear about the sort of model which they involve.

(a) THE THEORY STATED.

(1) *Infantile sexuality.* It seems clear that when Freud published his *Three Essays on the Theory of Sexuality* in 1905, he was suggesting answers to limited questions. He stated the problems very clearly in his *Outline of Psycho-analysis* in 1940 :

'(*i*) It is a remarkable fact that there are people who are only attracted by the persons and genitals of members of their own sex.

(*ii*) It is equally remarkable that there are people whose desires behave in every way like sexual ones, but who at the same time disregard the sexual organs and their normal use; people of this kind are known as "perverts".

(*iii*) And finally it is striking that many children (who are on that account regarded as degenerate) take a very early interest in their genitals and show signs of excitation in them.' (p. 10).

The 'remarkable' phenomena of homosexuality, perversions, and infantile sexuality, which Freud aimed to link together and explain by his theory, are not like parapraxes, hysterical fits or dreams in that they seem *prima facie* pointless or without standards or momentarily lapsing from recognized standards. A sexual pervert is not a man who bungles a performance any more than a homosexual is a man who acts haphazardly or in a dream state. Such behaviour presents an explanatory puzzle not because it exhibits no standards or objectives but because it exhibits 'remarkable' ones. Freud's theory showed the connexion between these types of behaviour by explaining how people come to have such odd standards and objectives.

Freud claimed that in the satisfaction of the main needs of hunger, thirst and elimination, a subsidiary form of 'organ-pleasure' was aroused which was centred around the erotogenic zones of the body—the mouth, the anus, and the genitals.   In time, activities like sucking and anal stimulation were performed because of the organ-pleasure derived from them quite irrespective of their initial function of removing intraorganic stimulation. Freud assumed a biological norm of development, the different erotogenic zones being sensitized in turn as the child moved through the famous oral, anal and phallic periods. In this manner the sex-instincts developed alongside the ego-instincts, each with their own somatic source and with their own peculiar satisfaction. These instincts worked independently at first and only came to work together in the final organization of the sexual function after puberty, in the usual sense of 'sexual'. Too little or too much satisfaction of any of these instincts could occasion 'fixation' at any of the stages; and this paved the way for sexual perversion—the concentration on the relevant form of organ-pleasure to the exclusion of its usual and subsidiary role in normal sexual intercourse.

(2) *The development of libido*. Freud has often been accused of developing an exclusively biological sort of theory, of ignoring the part played by relationships with others in developing odd interests and standards. This is an unjust accusation; for he advanced an elaborate and often extremely puzzling theory about the development of libido or sexual longing—'that force by which the sexual instinct is represented in the mind'. For though the child is auto-erotic at first, aiming at organ-pleasure from the different erotogenic zones, its love comes to be transferred to objects, like the mother, associated with organ-pleasure. Its love, too, is always ambivalent with hate which derives from the primal repudiation by the narcissistic ego of an object which is the source of alien stimuli. This love, however, may remain narcissistic, or directed towards the self, instead of anaclitic, with the mother as object-choice. Homosexuals, Freud suggested, have usually passed through an early stage of fixation on their mothers and have identified themselves with them, adopting for themselves the feminine role.

The development of libido reaches a culmination at about the age of four, when interest is centred predominantly on the genitals. This is the famous Oedipus phase. The boy wishes for sexual contact with his mother and develops as a rival of his father. The way in which the situation is resolved depends upon the degree to which masculinity or femininity (identification with the parent of the same or opposite sex) is developed in the boy or girl. For Freud postulated a fundamental bisexuality which does not necessarily follow the biological make up of the child. The child, depending on his sexual make up, can take either parent as a love object or identify himself or herself with either as an extension of narcissism and thus develop an ego-ideal. The way in which this Oedipus situation is resolved is crucial in the formation of the Super-ego of which the ego-ideal forms a part. For the child may take into itself both the normative demands and standards of the admired parent as well as the disapproval of his unacceptable wishes. In this way a precipitate is left in the Ego representing social traditions handed on by the parents.

(3) *The mechanisms of defence.* The relationships with parents determine not only the pattern of the child's attachments to others but also, on Freud's view, the type of technique he tends to adopt to deal with his own instinctual wishes. For his wishes for organ pleasure are not likely to be treated by his parents in the same way as his desire to eat or to play with bricks and beads. Few parents view with equanimity the child's delight in its own excrement, its masturbation, or quasi-sexual advances. This makes its natural desires dangerous and its secret pleasures taboo. So it deals with them by means of various *mechanisms*. It may *project* them or attribute them to the environment as when a child attributes hatred to its doll. It may *introject* its parent as a defence against losing a loved object and by taking into itself the parent's disapproval of its unacceptable wishes develop a strong *reaction-formation* against them—e.g. Puritanical disapproval of sexual activity.

In *rationalization*, objectionable instinctual demands are satisfied under the cloak of socially respectable reasons and in *sublimation* the object of an instinct is changed without blocking it. This enables sexual striving to be satisfied in a desexualized manner as in brotherly love. In *repression* a wish is not consciously put away as in denial or suppression; it passes out of consciousness and is prevented from re-entering consciousness. But it continues to exert an influence and the individual is often beset by anxiety, by fear to which no object can be attached. It can only emerge in a disguised form in dreams or trouble a man in the various parapraxes, neuroses, and psychoses. Repression is the most important of all the mechanisms; for Freud claimed that it is the basis of the unconscious. In his earlier work he thought that the unconscious is composed mainly of wishes that have been conscious but became repressed; in his later work he developed the view that part of the Id never reaches consciousness. It is held down by repression. Freud held that childhood wishes persist and exert an influence on adult behaviour. The mechanisms for dealing with them not only operate whenever they threaten, but also, starting from their operation at the period of infantile sexuality, set up habitual reactions which come to constitute a man's character.

(*b*) CRITIQUE OF THE THEORY. All sorts of queries could be raised about the truth of these speculations; but I am not here concerned with the truth of Freud's speculations—only with the *sort* of speculations they are. There are two main queries that arise in this context, the first in relation to the type of phenomena explained and the second in relation to the type of explanation offered.

(1) *The extent of the phenomena explained.* The first query is about the extent of the phenomena which Freud thought that he could explain in terms of infantile sexuality and the mechanisms of defence. He has often been credited with a preposterous pansexualism. But, as has been shown, he did distinguish the ego-instincts from the sex instincts and never thought that everything could be explained in terms of the sex instincts. His interest in them was aroused quite early on because, in his early work on the psycho-neuroses, he found that the root of the affections lay usually in the conflict between the claims of sexuality and those of the ego. He followed up Charcot's hunch expressed in his famous saying 'that certain nervous disorders are always a question of "la chose genitale" ' and found confirmation of it in most surprising places. His *Three Essays on the Theory of Sexuality* were the result.

But he did not confine his theory to the explanation of perversions and homosexuality. In his sensational *Character and Anal Erotism*, written in 1908, he claimed that people whose pleasure in anal sensations had been unusually great in infancy were apt to develop in later life a triad of character traits : orderliness, parsimony, and obstinacy. Such people had usually found pleasure in holding back their faeces in infancy, which was disapproved of; the character-traits were the result of the different mechanisms employed to deal with these dangerous wishes. Cleanliness and orderliness were reaction-formations against these infantile delights; interest in money was a sublimation, money being a substitute object; obstinacy was a continuation of reaction to parental insistence. Similarly sarcasm, scepticism and food faddism were regarded as oral traits; exhibitionism as a phallic one. Even curiosity was regarded as a sublimation of interest in the forbidden secrets of sex.

Now this is a highly ingenious and imaginative theory. But how far is it to be extended? Did he think that he was explaining *all* character-traits or only extreme types? In other words, did Freud imply that orderliness, parsimony, and obstinacy were *deviations* from an assumed norm? For he claimed that obsessionals manifest exaggerations of these traits just as schizophrenics manifest exaggerations of oral traits. His theory was that anal character-traits are produced by *fixation* at the anal stage of sexuality. Did he assume that those who were not fixated and who are reasonably tidy, careful with money, and determined, *also* developed these less exaggerated traits as a result of their reactions to toilet training? Did he suggest the same *sort* of explanation of their character-traits as he did of those who were over-tidy and obsessive? For there is surely a difference between being *trained* to follow rules of tidiness and economy and developing these traits as a reaction-formation against or a sublimation of dangerous wishes. These mechanisms seem to describe things that *happen* to a man, whereas when we speak of training we wish to bring out that the transaction is unlike that of being conditioned. A man who is trained is brought up to see the point of rules which form the basis of his habits. He will accordingly modify the rules according to differences in the situation where they have to be applied. A man who is conditioned, on the other hand, has some sort of regulatory mechanism stamped in to his behaviour in a manner which involves neither his co-operation nor his understanding; he will therefore follow rules in a rigid and unintelligent manner. The economy of a shrewd business man is very different from that of a miser. These very different sorts of character traits must have a very different type of genesis. It is not clear whether Freud thought that *all* character-traits were explained by his theory or only those that were in some way exaggerated or un-adapted to the social milieu in which the individual was brought up.[1]

The same sort of trouble is startlingly apparent in his theory of the Super-ego which purported to explain conscience and moral behaviour generally. It may well be that customary behaviour, or doing the done thing, is the product to a large extent of introjecting the demands of those admired figures with whom the child has identified himself (it could equally well be also a matter of spontaneous imitation). It is plausible, too, to suggest, as Freud did, that those who are over-scrupulous and obsessive about the performance of duties have been 'fixated' at a period in childhood or have introjected their parent's sadism towards them-selves or have turned inwards their own frustrated

---

[1] Ernest Jones claims that this is merely a matter of degree : Normal tidiness, he says, "is not simply the result of training but surely a defence of reaction against the universal anal erotism. The keen alpine climber may or may not display it in neurotic or compulsive form, but the source of his interest or drive can certainly be traced back to various infantile wishes in addition of course to the rational reasons. And we consider that the energy moving him comes ultimately from such unconscious sources".

aggression. But customary and obsessive behaviour is not morality; for by 'morality' we mean *at least* the intelligent following of rules the point of which is understood. A moral man may in general pay his debts and be punctual, but on occasions he will modify the general rule to a certain extent if the circumstances are exceptional. A man who just does the done thing or who is obsessive will conform either unthinkingly and unintelligently or in a manner which is grossly inappropriate to the situation. Freud dealt only with what Piaget in *The Moral Judgment of the Child*, called the 'transcendental' stage of conventional morality when standards are regarded as coming from an unquestionable external authority; his theory of the Super-ego fits this stage of development very well. But he says nothing of Piaget's 'autonomous' stage, when children come to see that rules are alterable and that they depend upon mutual consent. No doubt everyone carries round what Freud called a 'precipitate' of his early conditioning; but it is not clear whether Freud thought that *all* moral behaviour could be explained in this manner, or whether he thought his theory of the super-ego applicable only to exaggerated and unintelligent conformity with rules.

(2) *The model of explanation involved.* This problem of the extent of the phenomena explained by Freud is inseparable from the problem of the type of explanation involved. Are the mechanisms of defence properly termed 'mechanisms'? Do they refer to things that happen to a man which can be explained in mechanical terms and which cannot be described as intelligent or unintelligent? Or are they miscalled 'mechanisms'

because they are really techniques which conform to the rule-following purposive model of
behaviour?

A case can be made for saying that the same
dichotomy in models of explanation, which we have
noted in Freud's other explanations, is also to be found
in his account of the mechanisms of defence. He distinguished, for instance, between primary and secondary identification. As an account of what happens to
primary processes these mechanisms seem scarcely
intelligible—as could be expected. The child's primi-
tive way of dealing with its environment is to incorporate it through the mouth or to spit it out.
There is no distinction, therefore, in primary identification, between imitating the mother and swallowing
her, since, before the development of the ego, the child
cannot think of itself as separate from the external
world. Similarly primary projection is the earliest
form of rejection involved in spitting out what is
painful. Freud's account of these mechanisms as
characteristics of primary processes seems to mirror,
in mentalistic terms, processes that are purely
mechanical. They are like other happenings described
in his account of the vicissitudes of instincts. In dis-
placement, for instance, the current of energy involved in a wish gets attached to a substitute object;
it may also, if blocked in its flow towards the outside
world, turn round on the subject, as when aggression
turns inwards because it is ineffective in destroying
external objects; also, because of the ambivalence
of love and hate, the wishes involved may be reversed
into their opposite. These goings-on sound very odd
as descriptions of mental processes; and this is because

Freud was giving an account of what happens to a man in quasi-mechanical terms.

When, however, Freud talks of the mechanisms of defence as ego-functions or characteristics of secondary processes, the model seems very different. In secondary identification, for instance, the ego loves an object—e.g., the father or mother—which cannot be possessed and whose loss is dreaded. So it guards itself against loss of the loved object by introjecting it or taking it into itself in the form of an ego-ideal. This sounds quite a rational sort of move—rather like hanging the picture of a hero above the mantelpiece. Similarly, projection, as a secondary process, involves warding off threatening emotions or excitations, by attributing them to the environment. Rationalization, or satisfying objectionable instinctual demands under the cloak of socially acceptable reasons sounds like another intelligent dodge. So also does reaction-formation or setting up a permanent tendency to react against dangerous wishes. It sounds like a schoolboy's determination to think of Douglas Bader whenever he finds himself discouraged by failure. Finding a substitute object for forbidden wishes in sublimation, and letting them pass out of the mind in repression, sound like obvious techniques. It is as if Freud postulated a limited number of stratagems which are possible in a game whose point is to avoid a dangerous current; some come to favour one type of stratagem, others another; and these predilections become habitual. In the same way a man learning to drive might encounter a car coming round the corner on the wrong side and swerve to the left; this defence against danger gradually becomes habitual so that he develops a habit of keeping to the left when corner-ing. He might even, as in Freud's later account of anxiety, begin to feel uneasy long before coming to the corner, and hug the left hand side in anticipation. He has a reason for keeping to the left in the first place and this becomes built in as a permanent rule-following disposition. In a similar way, on Freud's theory, a Puritan would be a man who had built up a technique for dealing with dangers arising from his own wishes.

But this rational model of the acquisition of tech-niques does not really fit Freud's account of the mechanisms of defence and the way in which they pass into traits of character. For though they look like intelligent performances, they do not satisfy some of the relevant criteria. To start with, Freud did not think that the performer sees the point of the move even though it can be seen to be directed to-wards an end. Repression is different from denial or conscious suppression. It is something that seems to happen when confronted with a dangerous wish. It is not like putting a thought out of the mind; the thought just passes out of mind. Similarly a man who sublimates sexual desire by adopting the attitude of St. Francis to animals and men does not see the point of what he is doing. He just finds himself getting very attached to his dog. In projection a man who says that his wife is irritable does not realize that he is dealing with his own aggression towards her. Now it might be argued that a man who keeps to the left in going round a corner just finds himself doing this in a similar way. Perhaps ; but at some time he has seen the point of this if he has been trained in a technique. He could also tell anyone the point of doing this if asked. But a man who is sublimating has *never* seen the point of this and would not say, if questioned, that the point of loving his dog was to ward off troublesome sexual wishes.

This leads on to the second way in which the mechanisms are unlike intelligent stratagems which pass into habitual techniques. One of the criteria of a performance being intelligent is that the performer will vary it in accordance with changes in the situation. A man who has been trained to drive will, on occasions, where there are no hedges and where he can see the road ahead for miles, corner on the wrong side if he is in a hurry or if there is an uneven surface on the left hand side. He will vary the rule and even disregard it under certain conditions. But a Puritan will behave quite differently if his traits are the product of a reaction-formation against his sexual wishes. He will apply his code rigorously and in an undiscriminating manner. Guilt will attach even to his legitimate sex relations with his wife. He will accuse her of tempting him and read the Bible over her ravished body. Similarly, as has already been shown, a man who is rationalizing an unacceptable wish will not be affected by the adducing of any logically relevant considerations. He will remain quite imperious to changes in a situation, like a man under post-hypnotic suggestion.

Thirdly, one of the hallmarks of being trained in a technique is that there will be transfer of training of a kind that takes account of relevant differences. A man who has been trained to translate classical languages into English will also possess techniques for translating civil service jargon into English fit for public consumption. But a man who has reacted to toilet training by hoarding his faeces will, also, on Freud's view, generalize this habit and become parsimonious with money. This may be similar in that both forms of hoarding are ways of exerting power ; but the respects in which faeces resemble money are too remote to make the transfer look as if it involves much intelligence. There is a transfer to an object which, as Freud puts it, may be *emotionally* equivalent. But to say that it is equivalent in this respect is, more or less, to deny that it is similar in most other relevant respects.

The problem can be put succinctly. At one extreme there is what we call training, the typical example of which would be the handing on of a skill on some sort of apprenticeship basis. This would involve co-operation between the parties involved and explanation of the point of rules which are passed on and tried out in practice.   At the other extreme, would be dispositions inculcated by purely mechanical means— e.g., by drugs, brain surgery, or a rigorous and un-failing reward and punishment system. This could be called conditioning. The sorts of transactions which Freud describes occupy an indeterminate position between the two extremes. They look superficially like intelligent techniques; but a closer examination shows that they are unlike techniques in many re-spects. Yet they do not seem to be processes describ-able in purely mechanical terms like processes of the brain.

In this respect the mechanisms of defence against wishes are, in their operation, rather like the wishes

themselves. For, as has been shown, the concept of
'wish' is like and yet unlike the concept of 'his reason'.
Behaviour is directed towards a goal; yet it cannot be
regarded as intelligently so directed. The unconscious
processes involved conform to no logical or causal
canons of relevance; yet the goal is somehow arrived
at. Similarly the mechanisms of defence against
wishes are relatively effective in warding off or avert-
ing danger to the ego; yet the mechanisms involved
do not conform to criteria which would enable us to
describe them as intelligent performances.

Freud spoke of mental processes, especially in his
early work, in a language taken from the mechanical
descriptions of physiology. But, when he developed
his interest in ego psychology later on, he spoke increasingly in the 'as if' language based on a purposive
rule-following model. He speaks of the unconscious
as if a man were choosing means to some end dictated
by an unconscious wish. In his final work, his *Outline
of Psycho-analysis*, he said :

'We make our observations through the medium of
the same perceptual apparatus precisely by the help of
the breaks in the series of (conscious) mental events,
since we fill in the omissions by plausible inferences and
translate them into conscious material. In this way we construct, as it were, a series of conscious events comple-
mentary to the unconscious mental processes. The relative certainty of our mental science rests upon the
binding force of these inferences. Anyone who goes
deeply into the subject will find that our technique
holds its ground against criticism[1]. (pp. 18-19).

[1] Italics author's, not Freud's.

Perhaps Freud's lasting contribution to psychology lay not simply in the startling discoveries which he made, but also in showing, by implication, that neither the rule-following purposive model nor the mechanical model of explanation are really adequate for conceptualizing his revolutionary insights.

CHAPTER FOUR

DRIVE THEORIES

'For the possibility must be faced that the putting of
questions in the strategy and logic of general behaviour
analysis to rats can settle few such questions except for
rats.'   S. KOCH

Introductory

A GREAT deal of time has been spent on
Freud's theory—indeed many would say an in-
ordinate amount of time in a monograph of this
length. The justification of this is not simply the
intrinsic interest of his speculations, but also the fact
that he did work with human beings and produce
theories whose concepts went hand in hand with his
empirical findings. Most modern theories of motivation, by contrast, have been produced by people who
have mainly studied rats.

The point of devoting so much time and money to
the study of rats is not as clear-cut as it once was. In
the hey-day of behaviourism Hull, who exerted a great
influence on theorizing, quite clearly thought that a
deductive science could be developed in which the
rôle of the rat was rather like that of the ball rolling
down the inclined plane in Galilean mechanics. Rat
men nowadays are more cautious. They protest, when
pressed, that they are studying only the mechanisms
which underlie behaviour, or that they are only trying
to isolate very general conditions of all learning,
human and animal alike. But when the extrapolation

of concepts begins, it is only too easy to ignore
significant differences in the pursuit of suggestive
similarities. If, for instance, a theorist regards speech
as a series of stimuli, it is obvious from the start that
the theory of human behaviour which is likely ' emerge
is going to be riddled with conceptual confusion.

In this context Tolman, one of the early behaviourists, made a most significant admission whilst
confessing his faith. He said in 1938:

> 'Let me close, now, with a final confession of faith. I
> believe that everything important in psychology (except
> perhaps such matters as the building up of a super-ego,
> that is *everything save such matters as involve society and
> words*,)[1] can be investigated in essence through the con-
> tinued experimental and theoretical analysis of the
> determiners of rat behaviour at a choice point in a maze'
> (Tolman, 1938).

But what an empty confession of faith this is! For
what is there of importance in human behaviour
which does *not* involve society and words?[2] Men are
born into a social environment; social norms confront
them from the start 'comme les choses', as Durkheim
said. Men, as Kant said, are part of nature in that they
act in accordance with laws. If a man falls off a cliff

---

[1] Italics author's, not Tolman's.

[2] Cp. a most suggestive passage from Wittgenstein's *Philosophical
Investigations:* 'One can imagine an animal angry, frightened, unhappy,
happy, startled : But hopeful? And why not? A dog believes his master
is at the door. But can he also believe his master will come the day
after to-morrow? And *what* can he not do here? How do I do it? How
am I supposed to answer this? Can only those hope who can talk?
Only those who have mastered the use of a language. That is to say,
the phenomena of hope are modes of this complicated form of life.
(If a concept refers to a character of human handwriting, it has no
application to beings that do not write.)' [p. 174.]

his body behaves in accordance with the law of gravitation. But men differ from the rest of nature in that they understand some of the laws in accordance with which they act and act differently because of this understanding. They also act in accordance with a quite different set of laws—normative laws—which they themselves create. Men live by rules and conventions. They inherit traditions and are what they are because of an inescapable history. These traditions and conventions are written into their languages, which mark off for them things which must be noticed, done or not done. Their actions, as has been shown, are classified and described in terms of such conventions and are insufficiently described, let alone explained, in terms belonging to a different logical level. Rats, on the other hand, do not create institutions; they do not inherit traditions; they have no history. Tolman was therefore perceptive in seeing the dangers of extrapolating laws of rat behaviour to any human behaviour which involves society and words. But did he see the far-reaching implications of his admission?

The result of this frequent but too little considered jump from animal behaviour to human behaviour is conceptual confusion. Often concepts which *might* be applicable to the behaviour of rats under certain conditions—e.g. that of 'drive' or 'stimulus'—are transferred in a brisk and brazen way to the human level and we hear of 'the drive to know' and other such logical hybrids. Quite often, however, the reverse process occurs. In interpreting the behaviour of animals, experimenters use categories of description which are really only applicable to human beings. For instance we often speak of an animal 'wanting' something. Properly speaking the term 'want' implies that a person knows what he wants (McGuiness, 1957). When, however, we apply this sort of concept to animals we do so by tacitly withdrawing some of the conditions for using the word. Psychologists often assume that there is, as it were, a basic meaning for such words which applies universally to animals and men. When it is applied to men it is as if we implant a superstructure on the ground-plan of the term's meaning. But usually the process is quite the reverse. We have a term with a well-established use at the human level and withdraw a pillar or two when we apply it to animals. The danger is, in such analogical descriptions, that we bring about the complete collapse of the concept.

It is an interesting fact that those who have worked on rats and who have developed theories of motivation as a result, seldom speak of the 'motives' of the rat. This may be because of the verbal impropriety of talking in this way about rats. I suppose one might say of one of Kohler's apes: 'What was its motive for examining that box? Was it sheer curiosity?' But usually such questions do not arise with animals in experimental situations. Their behaviour is not up for assessment. Speculation is concerned more with the mechanisms underlying behaviour than with what the animal is up to. Indeed experiments are carefully arranged so as to narrow down the possible goals, and to control the possible means to them. The problem is usually to determine the factors which affect the strength of persistence towards the goal or the choice of some paths rather than others on the way to it.

There is, as a result, a systematic ambiguity in talk

about theories of motivation. If, for instance, it is said that Freud produced a theory of motivation, the meaning would probably be that he explained a lot of things in terms of motives; that he suggested, in other words, a number of rather surprising goals towards which people's behaviour was directed—usually unconsciously. If, on the other hand, a modern psychologist speaks of a theory of motivation he is usually referring to higher level or to genetic speculations about why people have the goals they have or how they come to acquire an interest in them; why they are more interested in some rather than in others and why they vary in the vigour and persistence with which they pursue them. In other words, quite different sorts of questions are being asked—much more like the types of question that Freud was trying to answer in his theory of infantile sexuality and in his pleasure principle than in his theory of unconscious mental processes.

Given, then, that theories of motivation are concerned with questions about the *explanation* of directedness, there are two typical sorts of problems which have encouraged the use of the concept of 'drive'. There is the problem in what is called instrumental learning of why it is that successful acts— i.e. acts that in fact help to bring about the goal— tend to be repeated or 'learnt'. There is also the problem of accounting for variations in the strength and persistence of directed behaviour which cannot be explained purely in terms of the variations of the incentive—e.g. the amount of food to be obtained. There is then the problem of the underlying mechanisms which has encouraged psychologists to look for some sort of efficient cause within the organism. In all this some theorists have forgotten, so it seems, that even if it is, on general logical grounds, appropriate to ascribe a motive to a rat, this must *at least* be a way of indicating the goal towards which its behaviour is directed. Brown (1953) and Farber (1954), for instance, go so far as to equate 'motive' with 'drive', a term used to designate the general function of energizing a response without, on their theory, any implications of directedness. This type of term is deliberately contrasted with terms like 'habit' and 'reaction-tendency' which, on their view, imply steering and directedness. This widespread and regrettable tendency to treat the concepts of 'motive' and of 'drive' as being more or less synonymous has added to rather than diminished the confusion about the sorts of questions that are being asked. But it is instructive to study in some detail how this strange conceptual metamorphosis has come about.

I *The types of question answered by the original concept of 'drive'*

Drives, it seems, were conceived as a result of the marriage between mechanical and purposive theories which took place during the period between the two world wars. They contained features of both parents— the suggestion of striving together with that of push from behind favoured by mechanical theorists since Descartes. Tough-minded behaviourists were thus free without loss of face to entertain elements of purposive theories; for the metaphysical *hormé* or will to live now appeared as a series of scientifically respectable efficient causes.

(a) TOLMAN: Tolman, for instance, in his *Purposive Behaviour in Animals and Men*, introduced the concept of 'drive' to refer to states of tension which initiate directed behaviour. McDougall's instincts were ruthlessly scrutinized and, where an innately determined demand for a goal object could reasonably be postulated, together with definite initiating physiological conditions, first-orders drives were said to exist. For instance, in food-hunger, after periods without nourishment, there was said to be an initiating physiological state of disequilibrium in the nutritive alimentary system. This released a demand for alimentary satiation plus an innate 'expectancy' that certain types of object (e.g. the nipple) are appropriate ways of getting to satiation, or physiological quiescence. Tolman postulated such drives to account for the *activation* of the demands for various goal-objects. He did not put forward a drive-reduction theory of re-inforcement. By this is meant that he did not use the concept of 'drive-reduction' to translate Thorndike's assumption put forward in his 'law of effect' that goal-directed sequences are *built up* or *acquired* because of the satisfaction obtained by attaining a goal of a certain sort. Indeed he was very critical of the 'law of effect' and gave much weight to the evidence of latent learning—of things that are learnt without any kind of reward or punishment. On his view demands for objects were either innately determined or acquired in accordance with other principles of learning—especially the frequency with which a means object has been found to lead on to a goal. Conditions of drive either only *activated* behaviour cycles or determined *selectivity*, the emphasis of parts of the environment to the exclusion of others.

But why did Tolman employ the concept of '*drive*' to account for this activation and sensitization of perceptual expectancies and motor sets? Many would say that it was a culture-bound concept, peculiarly suited to the American way of life. But a more satisfactory explanation is in terms of Tolman's behaviourist allegiance and his horror of the untestable speculations of purposivism. McDougall, for instance, seemed to assume that animals had foresight of the ends towards which they were impelled by some inner entelechy rather like Aristotle's efficient cause. The ghost of the ideo-motor theory—that action is initated by a picturing of the end—haunted his theory. Tolman's drives laid the ghost and made the most of both worlds. For like Hobbes' old concept of 'endeavour' (Peters, 1956) they conveyed the impression of purposive striving ; yet they explicitly referred to efficient causes of a tough-minded physiological sort. And if the actual states of tension or disequilibrium seemed difficult to observe, Tolman could always have recourse to the methodological move, which he himself did so much to popularize, that drives were 'intervening variables' correlating variations in selectivity and persistence towards a goal with variations in antecedent conditions like food-schedules.   Thus ' drives ' for Tolman acted as a bridging concept between purposivism and traditional behaviourism. They were efficient causes; yet their very name suggested directedness.

(*b*) HULL: Hull, the most influential of all drive theorists, used the concept rather differently from Tolman. He introduced it as an additional mechanical concept to deal with certain deficiencies in the theory of conditioned responses which he took over from Watson and Pavlov. This theory employed a simple mechanical model of explanation as old as Descartes and Hobbes. It postulated built-in sensori-motor connections such that any stimulus sets up some sort of agitation in the sense-organ which transmits impulses *via* the nervous system to the muscles, and thus automatically brings about movements. When another stimulus is presented together with the original stimulus (the bell as well as the plate of food), through the formation of sensori-motor connexions, it comes to set off movements even in the absence of the original stimulus. The movements in question were preparatory movements like those of salivation, rather than the actual movements set in motion by the food or unconditioned stimulus. Nevertheless they were sufficiently closely related to the movements associated with eating for it to be said that the bell became a signal for food. The food, too, acted as a *reinforcement* of the conditioned response as the latter could be 'extinguished' if no reinforcement followed.

Pavlov's 'law of reinforcement' was formulated about the same time (about 1900) as Thorndike's 'law of effect'. Their similarity has often been noted, though Thorndike's law explained something rather different, namely instrumental learning. Pavlov's conditioned responses were, as it were, preparatory movements in relation to the goal of eating, but were not instrumental to attaining it. The food was presented to the dog; the dog did not have to learn movements to obtain it. Thorndike's cats, on the other hand, learned movements which enabled them to obtain food by escaping from a box. He postulated that successful movements were stamped in by the satisfaction which followed them.

Both Thorndike's law of effect and Pavlov's law of reinforcement stated a more or less brute matter of fact connexion between preparatory and instrumental movements and the unconditioned stimulus and satisfaction which followed. But neither of them developed anything in the way of a serious theory to explain why this happened. Pavlov, it is true, spoke of 'irradiations' in the brain and Thorndike made some rather general speculations about 'confirmatory reactions' being controlled by large fractions of the higher levels of the cortex. But these were only theories about the underlying mechanisms. Hull tried to provide a theory of the mechanical type which would accommodate instrumental learning in the framework of classical conditioning theory. To do this he added postulates of motivation to supplement the usual contiguity, frequency, and recency postulates of traditional associationism. But he translated these motivational postulates into mechanical terms since, being a behaviourist, he found mentalistic terms like 'satisfaction', which were associated with Thorndike's law of effect, particularly obnoxious. In his *Principles of Behaviour*, therefore, he introduced the concept of 'need' as a preliminary to introducing the more mechanical concept of 'drive'.

> 'When a condition arises for which action on the part of the organism is a prerequisite to optimum probability of survival of either the individual or the species, a state of need is said to exist' (p. 57).

These needs bring about internal stimulation which is

removed by motor activity. So a connexion is strengthened when a stimulus and a response occurs together and some *internal* stimulation is thereby reduced. Hull introduced the concept of 'drive' as an intervening variable to link observable events—e.g. variations in eating—with antecedent conditions—e.g. number of hours since the intake of food. He was thus able to formulate his 'law of reinforcement' corresponding to Thorndike's 'law of effect':

> 'Whenever a reaction takes place in temporal contiguity with an afferent receptor impulse resulting from the impact upon a receptor of a stimulus energy, and this conjunction is followed closely by the diminution in a need (and the associated diminution in the drive, and in the drive receptor discharge) there will result an increment in the tendency for that stimulus on subsequent occasions to evoke that reaction' (p. 71)

This principle explained both the strengthening of built-in connexions and the setting up of new ones by conditioning.

But needs and drives were not postulated by Hull to account simply for the *acquisition* of habits; they also explained the *utilization* of habits in performance as in Tolman's theory. In his 6th postulate Hull claimed that 'Associated with any drive is a characteristic drive stimulus whose intensity is an increasing monotonic function of the drive in question' and in his 7th postulate that 'Any effective habit strength is sensitized into reaction potentiality by all primary drives active within an organism at a given time . . .' Reaction-potential is, in other words, a product of both drive and strength of habit.

This is interesting in that it indicates both the

ubiquitousness of drives on Hull's theory and their mechanical properties. Indeed it is difficult to see sometimes quite why Hull needs the concept of 'drive' as well as of 'need' unless it is to stress the mechanical model. Koch rightly refers to the relationship between 'drive' and 'need' as 'one of the enigmas of *Principles of Behaviour*. (Koch, 1954). But though a fog of conceptual obscurity shrouds the relationship, it is obvious enough that Hull employs the concept of 'drive' to present a mechanical picture of the operation of needs. He says, for instance,

'Animals may almost be regarded as aggregations of needs. The function of the effector apparatus is to mediate the satiation of these needs. They arise through progressive changes within the organism or through the injurious impact of the external environment. The function of one group of receptors (the drive receptors) is to transmit to the motor apparatus, via the brain, activating impulses corresponding to the nature and intensity of the need as it arises. Probably through the action of these drive receptors and receptor-effector connexions established by the processes of organic evolution, the various needs evoke actions which increase in intensity and variety as the need becomes more acute' (p. 65).

The apparatus of drive-receptors and drive-stimuli, which, to put it mildly, is highly conjectural, preserved the picture of impulses being transmitted internally to parallel the model of external stimulation.

II *The appropriateness of the early theories*

Hull's concept of 'drive' can be criticized from many points of view. Its *formal* position as an intervening variable, for instance, is indeterminate. It is not properly tied down to an independent variable, as Koch has shown. (1954). The *empirical* status of his 7th postulate, which states that reaction potential is a product both of drive and of habit strength, is also very shaky; for it seems to be a principle of unrestricted generality based on one series of experiments by Perin—on rats, needless to say.

But, nevertheless, Hull's treatment of motivation has its points. For he was clear about the questions that he was answering. He explicitly used the concept of 'drive' to answer two different questions. In the first place he used it in his statement of the law of reinforcement to explain the *acquisition* of habits. In the second place he used it, like Tolman, to explain the strength and selectivity of *performance*. It is important to distinguish these two different types of phenomena that require explanation; for it seems that many have assumed that if some such principle as the law of effect is operative in learning, then some similar drive-reduction explanation must also be postulated for the activation of a habit once acquired. Yet there are no good grounds for assuming that this must be so. Similarly Tolman's view is interesting in showing that it is quite possible to reject the law of effect as an explanation of the acquisition of habits, but to insist on some sort of drive explanation for the activation of habits once acquired. The question, however, which concerns us here is whether the concept of 'drive' is *logically* appropriate to explain *either* type of phenomenon.

(*a*) SPECULATIVE STATUS OF DRIVES AS INTERNAL STIMULATION: Whatever the protestations about 'drives' being intervening variables, it is clear that both Tolman and Hull conceived of them as more than convenient symbols for linking antecedent conditions with consequent conditions. Tolman made explicit mention of initiating physiological conditions and Hull introduced the apparatus of 'drive receptors' and 'drive stimuli' to suggest a picture of the causal mechanisms involved. Indeed the ambiguous status of Hull's theoretical constructs in respect of the substantial assertions which they imply about 'substructural detail' has been one of the most frequent criticisms of Hull's theory. (Koch, 1954). And, of course, the existence of such mechanisms, in the form which Hull's language suggests, is pure speculation. Skinner, for instance, claimed that it was a great mistake to treat drive as a *stimulus*, to identify the hunger drive, for instance, with stimuli arising from stomach contractions. Actually he claimed that the hunger drive can remain at a high level after eating has brought about the termination of such contractions and there is little evidence to assume that there are similar stimuli for other drives —e.g. the maternal drive. Also, as I have pointed out in relation to Freud's stimulation theory, the experimental evidence suggests that internal stimulation of the sort postulated by Tolman and Hull cannot even be a necessary condition of the activation of habits like eating and drinking, which are the very performances where the suggestion of internal stimulation is most plausible. And yet, without these speculations about internal causal mechanisms, what is the point in retaining the concept of 'drive'?

Nissen thoroughly debunks the mechanistic associations of the term 'drive' and suggests that it

refers only to the 'collective sensitization of a constella-
tion of acts which are related in so far as they tend to
produce a certain alteration in the organism or in one
of its relationships to the environment.' (Nissen, 1954).
Yet he retains the concept of 'drive' in spite of the
misleading associations to which it is bound to give
rise. A concept like that of 'sensitization' would do
just as well and would reflect more adequately the
state of our empirical knowledge. For all that has
been established to date is that there are a variety of
conditions such as deprivation and glandular secretion which *predispose* organisms to be sensitive to
specific types of object and to direct their behaviour
towards them. Such conditions may also facilitate
learning. But there are all sorts of *different* conditions.
Thyroid secretions, for instance, affect the vigour and
persistence of performance; but, even at the physiological level these are very different from conditions
like the state of the adrenal cortex which probably
influences the directedness of an animal's behaviour
when it is in search of salt water. The need, surely, is
to distinguish such conditions, to sort out carefully
the sorts of questions to which they seem to be
relevant. The trouble about the concept of 'drive' is
that it tends to lump together these conditions in
terms of a misleading mechanical model.

(b) THE SUGGESTION OF IMPULSION AND OF
SUFFICIENT CONDITIONS: The suggestion, too, of the
term 'drive' is that such predisposing conditions are
sufficient to explain the activation of the goal-directed
sequences in question. For surely this is the implication of saying that a person is 'driven' to act. Yet even
when account has been taken of habit-strength, such

predisposing conditions are, as a matter of fact, seldom sufficient. For there must usually also be *eliciting* conditions in the external environment as well as predisposing conditions determining sensitization. Under certain extreme conditions, perhaps, such directed sequences may be elicited by almost any object. Lorenz, for instance, has shown that under conditions of extreme sexual deprivation the copulatory act of certain species of birds may be elicited even by the experimenter's finger. In such cases, given that there is some innate or acquired pattern of response, the predisposing conditions seem sufficient to explain its activation. But *all* motivated behaviour is not like the case of a man who eats his hat. Yet to speak of such predisposing conditions as conditions of 'drive' suggests just this. For we say that a man is 'driven' to act when his actions are not in accordance with the logic of the situation, when, as it were, he is suffering from something rather than taking account of the situation in which he is placed. In such cases we regard either the predisposing factors or the external stimulation as *sufficient* to explain what happens. Either the man has no reasons for acting like this or his reasons are rationalizations. He is properly described as 'driven' to act; for 'drive' suggests not simply predisposing conditions, but impelling conditions which render what he does unavoidable. Nissen exposes the

'very old and still prevalent superstition inherent in the word "drive", that the organism is driven and guided to certain external goals, such as money or murder, by a mysterious force or homunculus who sits somewhere inside, preferably in the heart or brain.'

There may be such a superstition associated with the use of the word; but it dramatizes the suggestions in the proper use of the word that a man's directed behaviour can be *sufficiently* explained in terms of its antecedent causes, that his reasons make no difference to what he does, and that he can't help doing what he does. There *are* occasions when this concept is appropriate, e.g. in obsessive behaviour. But if the term 'drive' is used as a general concept to refer to *all* predisposing conditions, it has the effect of lumping together all motivated behaviour under a concept which is relevant to explain motivated behaviour under very special conditions. It thus impedes the special study of the types of condition which must hold when a man is *properly* said to be *driven* to act. For the omnibus use of the concept of 'drive' tends to prevent distinctions being made in the sort of questions that theorists are trying to answer. The thesis of this monograph is that the failure to make these sorts of distinctions stultifies most current theories of motivation.

(*c*) OBJECTIONS TO WHOLE CONCEPT OF STIMULATION: There is, however, a more deep-seated trouble about the concept of 'drive' in that it may involve an unlimited extension of the concept of 'stimulation', which is a causal concept that applies properly to the mere transmission of movements. It is adequate only at a certain level of description where questions about intelligent or unintelligent, correct or incorrect, do not arise. But both the phenomena of learning and of performance, which are the *explicanda*, can be appropriately characterized in both these ways. That is why theories employing the mechanical model of stimulation are inappropriate as explanations of what men do as distinct from what happens to them.

(i) *Intelligent actions cannot be sufficiently explained in causal terms:* Consider, first, the difficulties stemming from the fact that behaviour can be appropriately described as intelligent or unintelligent. It has been argued that the concept of 'end' or 'goal' is correlative with that of 'means'. We call something a goal not because it is a natural terminating point of movements but because movements persist towards it and vary in accordance with perceived changes in it and in conditions that lead to it. This adaptiveness or relevant variation in relation to change is also part of what we mean by 'intelligence'. That is why the concepts of 'intelligence' and of 'goal-directedness' are inseparable. Now the stimulus theorists tried to explain both the acquisition of such sequences and their activation once acquired in purely causal terms. But would it be appropriate to say even of Pavlov's dog that its salivation was caused by the sound of the bell? For this suggests that the salivation was a re-action to a stimulus, that it was a movement simply correlated with another movement. Yet experiments on extinction suggest that even a response at this level was not unintelligent; for the dog came to change it in the light of differences in the situation. Even the early behaviourists gave up the concept of 'reflex' which suggested a full-blooded causal transaction. For a response is something that is made *to* or *in the light of* a situation. It is not simply a movement caused by another movement. Skinner, a later behaviourist, went even further than this in implicitly abandoning the causal model. For he distinguished 'operant' from 'respondent' responses. 'Operant' responses were those which cannot be correlated with any known stimuli. Indeed he held that the stimulus conditions are largely irrelevant to a proper understanding of these responses which, roughly speaking, cover the class of what we have called human actions.

The point, of course, is not that dogs are to be credited with unsuspected depths of foresight and insight into situations when they salivate or hide a bone. It is rather that the causal type of explanation is logically unsuitable to explain what a dog does, in so far as it shows intelligence. For the *explicandum* can only be adequately described by means of concepts like 'relevance' and 'appropriateness' to an end. Processes, on the other hand, like the melting of ice or the movements of glass when struck by a stone do not require such concepts for their description. They just happen. They are not recognized or described in terms which relate them to some kind of means-end nexus. For they do not vary in the light of situations related in this sort of way to them. They therefore can be sufficiently explained in causal terms.

If the mechanical picture of stimulation is insufficient to explain even the paradigm cases of behaviourist metaphysics, there is little virtue in extending it to cover other transactions as well. Yet this is what Hull obviously intended to do. He claimed (1943) that

'an ideally adequate theory even of so-called purposive behaviour ought, therefore, to begin with colourless movement and mere receptor impulses as such, and from these build up step by step both adaptive and maladaptive behaviour'.

His concepts of 'drive-receptor' and 'drive-stimulus' were attempts to implement this programme. But, as I have argued elsewhere (Peters, 1957), he never really began to tackle the difficulties of carrying out a programme which was in fact logically impossible. For, as soon as he started developing explanations instead of making merely programmatic announcements, a strange discrepancy developed between his theoretical definitions of constructs like 'stimulus' and 'response' and his actual descriptions of behaviour. R, for instance, which should refer only to colourless movements, designated *actions* like ' biting the floor-bars' and 'leaping the barrier', which are movements classified in terms of their end-results.

Not all drive theorists have accompanied Hull on his metaphysical pilgrimage. Tolman, for instance, claimed that the concept of behaviour was irreducible to that of movements at the physiological or reflex level. An act of behaviour, he claimed, has distinctive properties of its own—its goal-directedness, for instance, and its use of environmental supports as means objects towards a goal—which can be described irrespective of the muscular and neural processes underlying it. In this respect Tolman's account of behaviour was very similar to what has been previously referred to as the purposive rule-following model.

(ii) *Learning and performance involve standards of correctness :* Oddly enough, too, another modern behaviourist—Guthrie—has made much of the second main difficulty above the over-all use of the concept of stimulation. Hull used mechanical concepts to explain both learning or the acquisition of habits and performance. Now an obvious point to make about both the concepts of 'learning' and of 'performance' is that they both presuppose standards of *correctness*. A man who learns something is a man who comes to get something *right*. This notion of correctness applies partly to what is considered to count as a goal, as we have seen in obvious cases like that of signing a contract or getting married. It also applies to what are considered to be legitimate means or ways of getting to the goal which must conform to standards of correctness as well as of efficiency. If an action has been performed it must make sense to ask whether it was done correctly, skilfully, and so on—i.e., whether it conforms to standards which are involved in its being called an action of a certain sort. Similarly to learn to do something implies the attaining of the required standards by trial and error, insight, and various other postulated methods. Now if a rat is placed in a maze in a typical experiment on learning, the experimenter has already imposed the normative means-end framework on a food-seeking situation. By carefully constructing and controlling an artificial environment he makes it possible for his system of description to have a more or less unambiguous application. He can thus study the conditions which facilitate learning and which activate the required performances. What is called a correct response depends largely on the pattern of norms and means-end connexions by use of which he interprets what he sees. Thus he may be able to enunciate certain necessary conditions which determine the animal's learning or 'getting it right', in terms of predisposing and eliciting conditions. He may also be able to give sufficient explanations in causal terms for breakdowns in performance or in learning. But it is difficult to see how he can give a *sufficient* explanation of learning or performance in these sorts of terms. For there is no valid deduction of the normative standards necessary to define 'learning' or 'performance' from statements describing only causal conditions. Theories of learning are, in this respect, in a similar predicament to theories of perception so admirably illustrated by Hamlyn in the first monograph in this series. (Hamlyn, 1957).

(iii) *Guthrie's attempt to describe behaviour in terms of mere movements:* Now Guthrie saw this difficulty and accordingly made much of the distinction between 'movements' and 'acts'. 'Acts', he claimed quite rightly, are classes of movements defined in terms of their effects or outcome, and involves reference to concepts like 'success' and 'accomplishment', which are inappropriate at the level of mere movements. But instead of drawing the obvious conclusion that behaviour cannot be described let alone sufficiently explained in terms of mere movements, he claimed that psychology should concern itself *only* with the study of movements, especially those within the organism.

This was a heroic programme. But it ran into insoluble problems of description. Responses were viewed just as effector activities like the contraction of muscles and the secretion of glands. But how was a response to be *recognized* as being one of a certain sort? For such recognition was essential for his theory which maintained that an animal will do in a situation what it did before in a similar situation. Guthrie and Horton devized an ingenious experiment which supported their theory and their reductionist programme quite well, precisely because it represented a very special sort of learning situation. They placed cats in a puzzle box, release from which was obtained by touching a pole in the middle of the floor. They photographed the movements of the cats and found a remarkable repetition of movements in that the cats tended to repeat the posture in which they had first touched the pole and obtained release. Similar movements were those postures which the experiments agreed to be similar. But this was a very odd sort of learning situation. For *any* sort of touch deflected the pole and brought about the opening of the door ; it was very difficult for the cats to *avoid* touching the pole; and there was no discernible relationship between moving the pole and opening the door either in terms of visible connexion or in terms of variations of the way in which the door opened which could have been correlated with different ways in which the pole was touched. The experiment only established that animals will tend to adopt stereotyped methods of dealing with situations which require no intelligence. Thorndike's cats, who were placed in situations requiring intelligence, behaved very differently. Guthrie claimed to define the cat's behaviour in terms of movements and posture, rather than in terms of the effect of pole deflecting. But this was only possible because in situations which occasion stereotyped behaviour one of the many possible ways of bringing about a result tends to be repeated. It showed nothing about the possiblity of reducing *all* behaviour to movements. Indeed all it showed was the lengths of artificiality to which an experimenter has to go in order to give any plausibility to such a reduction.

(*d*) THE PROBLEM IS TO DECIDE WHEN THE STIMULA-
TION MODEL IS APPROPRIATE: The line of argument
here developed does not, of course, mean that the
mechanical model beloved by stimulus theorists is
never appropriate. It means that the problem is to
find out when it *is* appropriate rather than to assume
that it is always or never so. For instance, some model
such as this might well explain the activation of
sucking movements when they occur in an environmental vacuum after a stated number of hours of
food deprivation. Similarly, as has been argued
before, some such model might be sufficient to explain
tropisms or completely sterotyped instinctive patterns
which occur low down on the phylogenetic scale, or
breakdowns in performances at higher levels. The
basic error of theorists in psychology is to assume that
the *same* type of explanation can be used for a variety
of quite different kinds of phenomena. The concept of
'drive', in so far as it employs the mechanical model
of stimulation, has therefore the effect of blurring
important distinctions by assimilating all behaviour
to a type which seldom occurs—at least amongst men.

III *The Generalization of the concept of 'Drive'*

In its early days the concept of 'drive' was used to
answer relatively restricted questions. Indeed one
of the merits of Hull's use of the concept was that it
gave false answers to limited questions. But un-
fortunately the concept of 'drive', like that of 'the
unconscious', was taken up by others who extended
it in a manner more characteristic of metaphysical
than of scientific thinking.

(a) THE DOLLARD AND MILLER EXTENSION: The first sort of extension was to use the concept to refer indiscriminately to either internal or external stimulation. Dollard and Miller, for instance, held that 'Strong stimuli which impel action are drives. Any stimulus can become a drive if it is made strong enough. The stronger the stimulus, the more drive function it possesses'. A loud noise as well as a hunger pang could now be referred to as a drive. But if a noise is not too loud it is merely a cue[1]; presumably so also is a hunger twinge. The cue function of a stimulus depends upon its distinctiveness, the drive function on its strength. Now etymologically and in relation to ordinary use there is something to be said for linking the concept of 'drive' with that of impulsion. Indeed it is this implication of using the word that occasioned me to object to it as a *general* concept for referring to predisposing conditions. And there are occasions when we *need* to say that a man is driven to act, that he is impelled by stimuli like electric shocks and violent internal pains. But Dollard and Miller held that drives *always* function when a person learns or performs. For instance, in their celebrated example of the girl looking for a piece of candy under a book, the experimenters had to be sure that she wanted the candy. Otherwise they could not study the conditions which facilitate learning. But ' wanting candy ' was broken down into a general hunger drive and a more specific one for candy. To explain her behaviour

[1] The term "cue" begs all the same sorts of questions as the term "stimulus". It is, however, a more slippery term; for its indeterminacy enables those who like it to slither about between a causal and a purposive, rule-following model.

secondary drives related to social participation and social approval had also to be postulated. So she was 'impelled' to respond to certain cues which she met with in the room; the cues goaded her as well as guided her.

Now we do speak of people acting ' on impulse ' when they act without premeditation. In such cases causes like upsurges of emotion are *sufficient* to explain what they do. But not all cases of acting are particular cases of acting on impulse. Indeed the phrase 'acting on impulse' only has meaning in *contrast* to more usual ways of acting. The generalization of the model is another case of blurring important distinctions. Yet, perhaps, it was necessary; perhaps, like many metaphysical models it was illuminating in drawing out the logical implications of a concept on a large scale. It thus reveals in a glaring manner the inappropriateness of the model of impulsion, and hence, *a fortiori*, of the generalized concept of 'drive'. But it also obscures the important question of when a man may properly be said to be driven to act.

(*b*) 'ACQUIRED DRIVES': Another way of extending the concept of 'drive' was to postulate 'acquired drives'—for social approval, money, and the presence of company. Tolman, for instance, spoke of second-order drives like curiosity, gregariousness, and self-assertion. Yet he admitted that their existence was very hypothetical. For what evidence is there in such performances for the existence of initiating states of tension or terminating states of quiescence? Their connexion, too, with first-order drives was an unsolved problem. It still is, in spite of a spate of discussion about whether acquired drives are 'functionally autonomous' or in some way dependent on the basic homeostatic drives. The truth of the matter is that there is practically no concrete evidence to support Hull's general thesis about performance that reaction-potential is *always* a function of drive in the sense in which he conceived of 'drive'.

Many drive theorists, like Brown, have realized this:

'We might advance more rapidly if we were to start afresh and to deny at the outset that each and every object or situation for which an organism has learnt to strive must be accompanied by a characteristic acquired drive for that object' (Brown, 1953).

This is very revealing in that it makes explicit the generalization of the concept current in drive theory —the postulation of the drive-reduction sandwich to include *all* directed behaviour. But Brown, having seen the light, does not proceed to abandon the concept of 'drive' as a useful over-all concept. Instead he embarks on the metaphysical strategy of keeping the concept but rendering the theory irrefutable. He proceeds :

'One possible solution to our problem is to assume that the important motivating component of many of the supposed acquired drives for specific goal-objects is usually a learned tendency to be discontented or distressed or anxious in the absence of these objects. On this view, stimulus cues signifying a lack of affection, a lack of prestige, insufficient money, etc. would be said to acquire, through learning, the capacity to arouse an anxiety reaction having drive properties. This learned anxiety would then function to energize whatever behaviour is directed towards goal-objects by stimuli, and its reduction, following the achievement of those goals, would be powerfully re-inforcing '

I

This postulation of vague states of anxiety initiating a variety of goal-directed sequences is a far cry from the more precise, if mistaken, assumption of Hull about drive stimuli. Its obvious difficulties have been abundantly exposed[1]. It is interesting in that it illustrates the tendency of a theory to degenerate into metaphysics when its more precise assumptions have been challenged. For the description of the initiating state necessary for drive theorists has now been rendered so general as to be almost irrefutable. Approach behaviour—e.g. towards money, companionship, prestige—is described in terms of its correlative negative—e.g. the *avoidance* of conditions in which these commodities are absent. These conditions of deficit are then conceived of as being conditions of tension or anxiety, and the behaviour which attains the required goal can be conceived of as a case of drive-reduction. One by one the postulated conditions for the existence of drives have been withdrawn. We are left with vague states of anxiety which are presumed to initiate directed sequences, for the main reason that avoidance behaviour can be more plausibly poured into the empty mould of drive-reduction than approach behaviour

IV *Need-reduction*

The point has already been made that the relationship between 'drives' and 'needs' is obscure and that the concept of 'drive' seems to function as a method of translating the concept of 'need' into mechanical

[1] See, for instance, Harlow's and Nissen's comments in the same symposium, and those of Ritchie and Atkinson on Farber's *Anxiety as a Drive State* in the 1954 Nebraska symposium.

terms. It might well be said, therefore, that most of the obnoxious implications of drive-theories could be avoided if they were stated in terms of need-reduction. This would link the main theory of motivation of the present day with other theories like that of Lewin, who used the concept of 'need', and with a great amount of more piecemeal work done in the field of motivation,—e.g. the genetic work done on the physiological determinants of primary needs (Morgan, 1950), the work by social psychologists like H. A. Murray and Kardiner on the acquisition of needs, and by Bruner and Postman on the effects of needs on perception. The concept of 'need' would thus be a central unifying concept in motivational psychology and the concept of 'drive' might disappear, like the Marxist concept of 'state'—'banished to the museum of antiquities side by side with the spinning wheel and bronze axe'.

There is something to be said for this suggestion provided that the term 'need' is used in a fairly specific sense and does not assume the role of a postulate in an over-all theory. The concept of 'need', as has been shown, implies that there is a state the absence of which is, or is likely to be, damaging to the individual in question. In other words it is inescapably *normative*, implying that something is wrong with a person if certain conditions are absent. It is not usually *explanatory* as reference to a need is usually a way of giving prudential advice—of *contrasting* what a man is in fact doing with what he ought to be doing. It calls attention to the discrepancy between what a person is in fact doing and the accepted content of the rule-following purposive model.

There are two main ways in which the concept of 'need' can become—or seem to become—explanatory. It can, first of all, be used as more or less synonymous with the concept of 'motive' in that it can indicate the lack or absence of conditions that persistent and directed behaviour is restoring. In other words the goal is simply described in terms of bringing about, or restoring, conditions whose absence is a necessary condition of the directed behaviour. To speak of such motives as *needs* merely emphasizes their importance. Often a certain amount of classification is involved in such theories of needs. H. A. Murray, for instance, in Ch. 2 of his *Explorations in Personality*, defines 'need' as a construct

> 'which stands for a force (the physico-chemical nature of which is unknown) in the brain-region, a force which organizes perception, apperception, intellection, conation and action in such a way as to transform in a certain direction an existing, unsatisfying situation' (p. 124).

Now as the determinants of the 'force' are, on his own showing, unknown, the cash value of this definition is to postulate that behaviour is organized and directed towards transforming an unsatisfying situation. His concept of 'need' is indistinguishable from the concept of 'motive'. He later proceeds to introduce a veritable galaxy of needs, significantly enough all completed by verbs after the preposition 'to'. Acquisition, for instance, is the need to gain possessions and property, to grasp, snatch or steal things, to bargain and gamble, to work for money or goods. Conservance is the need to arrange, organize, and put away objects, to be tidy and clean, to be precise. Superiority is the need to gain power over things and to gain approval. Autonomy is the need to resist influence or coercion. And so on. Particular goal-directed activities are simply classified in terms of more general aims. Calling them 'needs' serves mainly to emphasize their generality and importance in American society. It fills in the general goals necessary to give some kind of content to the rule-following purposive model. This is explanatory in the sense that explanations in terms of motives are explanatory. But it is not an explanation *of* motives.

The concept of 'need' becomes explanatory in a second sense when it seems to give an explanation *of* motives. In this case conditions of lack are restored but the restoration of these conditions is not part of what is meant by the goal in question. For if the concept of 'need' is to explain motivated behaviour, then the conditions restored or brought about by it must be independently defined—i.e. in terms other than those necessary to define it as a goal-directed piece of behaviour. This is another way of reiterating the distinction between 'goals' and 'end-states' which has previously been made. For instance, a deficit of anti-diuretic hormone may enhance sensitivity and persistence towards water in the case of the motive of thirst. But the restoration of this hormone deficit is not part of what is meant by thirst as a motive. Neither does thirst usually mean the tendency to restore a more general bodily condition like water in the body. It just means the tendency to persist towards the activity of drinking. A theory of needs which accounts for thirst simply in terms of the absence of opportunities to drink would not be explanatory of thirst as a motive but a description of it. It becomes explanatory when a theory emerges about the deficit states in the body restored by drinking. A theory of 'needs' which related such deficit states to variations in vigour and persistence of drinking would thus state necessary conditions of motivated behaviour, and hence help to explain it.

The concept of 'needs' as used in this second sort of explanatory theory also involves reference to some kind of norm like that of homeostasis or survival[1]. The deficit states are regarded as injurious to the organism which involves some reference to a normal or healthy state.   In the case of Hull's need-reduction theory it is quite clear that he assumed a Darwinian theory of survival interpreted in terms of Cannon's homeostasis. As Koch (1956) has so aptly put it: 'there was a time not too many years ago when a direct pipe-line extended between Cannon's stomach balloon and the entire domain of "motivational" psychology'. And Hull also assumed that both the acquisition of habits and performance could be, in part, explained by means of 'need-reduction' conceived of in terms of this model. Enough has been said to cast doubt on the applicability of homeostasis as an *over-all* principle. Some phenomena, including motivational ones, may be explained by reference to it; but the trend nowadays is to reject the assumption that it is relevant to all motivational phenomena. Harlow (1953) for instance, in his celebrated paper on *Mice, Monkeys, Men and Motives*, explicitly attacked

---

[1] See, for instance, Olds' definition of "need" as 'the absence of something which if persistent will terminate the life or health of the organism'. (Olds, 1955.)

the assumption that homeostatic types of explanation were relevant to *all* types of learning. The reference to survival as an over-all assumption does not help much either. For not all deficit states which are injurious to survival give rise to directed and persistent behaviour which restores them. To quote McClelland (1953) :

> "For example, it is now known that vitamin B_{12} is necessary for the production of erythrocytes, and without B_{12} the organism will suffer from pernicious anemia and die. Yet a person suffering from anemia of B_{12} deficiency behaves in no way like a motivated person, at least by any of the usual measures of motivation," (p. 15)

And this is not an isolated exception. McClelland then goes on to point out that satisfying some needs sometimes results in death, and that reference to biological needs can provide only a very partial explanation of the guiding and controlling of animal let alone of human behaviour.

One of the obvious reasons for this is surely that man's environment is to a large extent conventional or artificial. Social life is never, like the jungle life popularized by evolutionary theorists, a matter of mere survival; it is a matter of surviving in a certain sort of way. As Socrates put it :

οὐ γὰρ τὸ ζῆν περὶ πλείστου ποιητέον, ἀλλὰ τὸ εὖ ζῆν

Normative standards entirely define some of the goals to be explained, like passing an examination, and enter into the description even of those most intimately connected with mere survival, like eating, eliminating, and copulating. Means to such goals are seldom to be described purely in terms of efficiency;

they also involve canons of social appropriateness. Such standards are infinitely variable and alterable. To explain adequately behaviour in accordance with such standards, recourse must be made to history and to concepts like those of 'decision', 'tradition', 'correctness', and 'training', which belong to the rule-following purposive model. Psychologists who have worked mainly on rats have assumed that it is the complexity of human life which makes the application of the biological model of need-reduction so difficult to apply. Their critics, who have often, like Nissen and Harlow, worked mainly on monkeys, stress the importance of other determinants like external stimulation or the 'drive to know'. But the basic difficulty, which is involved in generalizing any simple mechanical, physiological, or biological model is a *logical* one. The verb 'to know', for instance, can hardly be used appropriately of monkeys. For it does not simply mean 'having an expectation'; it also involves things like being *correct* in the expectation which one has and having good *grounds* for it. And monkeys could only have good grounds for their beliefs in an analogical sense. The types of concept that belong to the rule-following, purposive model are irreducible to those which are not intimately bound up with standards and conventions. Any attempt to give a sufficient explanation of human behaviour in these logically different sorts of terms is therefore bound to be inadequate.

The foregoing considerations suggest that, though the term 'need' can be used in an explanatory manner, the concept of 'need ' is a very dangerous and ambiguous one, especially if it is used in any over-all theory. In the first place, there are the normative implications which are inseparable from the concept; in the second place, the term 'need' is used in quite different ways as an explanatory term. It can be used as more or less synonymous with 'motive'; and it can be used in the context of bodily needs to indicate possible necessary conditions of *some* motivated behaviour. But, even when used in the latter sense, a distinction must be drawn between necessary conditions of learning and of performance. As Olds (1955) puts it

> 'need-reduction and reward have neither identical definition nor covariance. There are certainly rewards which are not need-reductions. . . . Needs do not really enter in the control of behaviour, except in the long run through the mediation of natural selection' (p. 76).

In other words 'need-reduction' in this sense may be quite distinct from reward or reinforcement. It may also be a necessary condition of the *activation* only of some performances, not of all.

In view of these ambiguities in the concept of 'need' it is obviously unsuitable as an over-all motivational concept. It would be advisable to retain the term 'motive' when 'need' is equivalent to 'motive', and when the term 'need' is used to explain motivated behaviour it should be used with extreme caution and with due regard to what aspects of motivated behaviour are being explained. It certainly should not be used as an over-all concept to explain *both* the acquisition of motives *and* their activation.

CHAPTER FIVE

THE REGRESSION TO HEDONISM

'The new psychology intuitively disposed of instincts and painlessly disposed of hedonism. But having completed this St. Bartholomew-type massacre, behaviouristic motivation theory was left with an aching void.'

H. HARLOW

Introductory

THERE have been many recent criticisms of the classical drive theories but singularly few replacements on the same ambitious scale. This is a move in the right direction; for the main argument of this monograph has been that the attempt to provide an all-inclusive theory of motivation is mistaken. There is, however, discernible a certain trend in theorizing which has come about through the recognition that there are classes of phenomena that cannot be plausibly explained in terms of the avoidance or drive-reduction model of the classical theory. Animals, surprising to relate, sip sugar and solve problems when they are not hungry. They explore their environment with no definite goal in view; they have preferences for salt which are inexplicable in terms of drive-reduction. In other words they seem to do certain things just for the sake of doing them.

Now this seems scarcely a monumental revelation.

It has seemed, however, surprising to those steeped in the model of explanation favoured by drive theorists. Some have admitted the importance of these approach phenomena and have invented a new class of 'drive' to explain them. Others have postulated a new sort of omnibus end-state—self-actualization or self-realization. Both these attempts to explain the recalcitrant phenomena involve keeping the same model of explanation but stretching one of the concepts involved like that of 'drive' or 'end-state'. There are others, however, who have been so impressed by the phenomena and by the objections to drive-deduction types of explanation that they have resurrected hedonism. For do not the new class of phenomena show that animals, like men, seek pleasure as well as avoid pain? And do they not learn things because they are pleasant as well as because they remove a tension or diminish stimulation?

This transition from drive theory to hedonism is most instructive to study. For it seems odd that a theory as hoary as hedonism should be resurrected to explain phenomena which we meet with every day of our lives, especially in view of the fact that philosophers have ceased to regard hedonism as an *explanatory theory*. A brief account must therefore be given of the three main ways of dealing with these new phenomena. When the last way is reached, the resurrection of hedonism, it is hoped that a brief analysis of the concepts involved will show both why the new phenomena have encouraged a return to hedonism and why concepts like 'pleasure' and 'affective arousal' in fact seem to do so little work in modern versions of this ancient theory.

I *The drive to know*

Perhaps the range of phenomena which have aroused most universal interest are those which seem to be initiated by some kind of external stimulation. This has led to the postulation of exteroceptive drives to balance the emphasis of the classical theories on internal stimulation. Under this heading come patterns of behaviour referred to by names like curiosity, manipulation, play and tropisms. Work done on the exteroceptively elicited behaviour patterns of birds, fish, and insects—mainly by naturalists like Lorenz, Thorpe, and Tinbergen—has been extended to monkeys and apes. This has revealed that curiosity is not only inexplicable in terms of the homeostatic drives but is itself a sufficient explanation of exploratory and problem-solving activity. In fact Harlow claims that the usual rewards of food seem, if anything, to hinder rather than facilitate learning of this sort (Harlow, 1953a). Nissen (1954) agrees with Harlow's findings and postulates a special drive to know, to perceive, and to explore. He objects to distinguishing homeostatic drives from other sorts of drives as he claims that such drives are exercises of parts of the nervous system which, as a part of the body, has its homeostatic requirements like any other part.

> 'The sense-organs "want to see" and hear and feel just as much as the mouth or stomach or blood-stream "want to eat" or contract or maintain a certain nutrient balance. ... It is the function of the brain to perceive and know ... Is it then unreasonable to postulate a primary drive— a drive for one of the main organs of the body, the brain, to perform its function of perceiving and knowing. ...

The idea of a drive to perceive and to know may be stated more broadly: *capacity is its own motivation*. That is, capacity implies, or carries with it, the motivation for expression. The organism does anything that it can do' (pp. 300, 301).

Nissen is no doubt right about the facts; but his explanation of them seems to be conceptually rather confused—even after we have politely averted our gaze from conceptual outrages like ' sense organs "want to see".' For, in the first place, 'drive' is now being used so widely that it seems vacuous. He insists that the cash value of the term 'drive' is to refer to sensitizing factors. But if a *general* drive to perceive and know is postulated, *to what* is a man or ape sensitized? The answer can only be to anything that turns up. In the second place the phrase 'capacity is its own motivation' sounds cryptic and decisive. But what does it mean? To postulate a motive is to state an end towards which action is directed. If the action in question is simply exploring without any further end, it is odd to say that the capacity which is being exercised is motivated at all. Perhaps Nissen is making the common mistake of psychologists of presenting a vacuous explanation as a sort of shadow for conceptual analysis. The concepts of 'perceiving' and 'knowing' are interesting in that both are achievement verbs. They imply standards of correctness, the performance of a task. We would not understand what 'knowing' and 'perceiving' *meant* unless we also understood what it was like to have good grounds for a belief, to see something when something is really there, and to get things *right*. These particular capacities have ends, as it were, built into them. Perhaps

Nissen's pronouncement that "capacity is its own motivation" is, in the case of these particular capacities, merely a way of drawing attention to this *conceptual* point. In other words it is analysis, not explanation.

II *Growth motivation*

Another move away from drive-reduction is that of workers in the therapeutic field who frankly wish to turn psychology into a sort of social technology, on the odd assumption that their findings might have relevance to the long-scale promotion of 'the good life'. Maslow (1955), for instance, uses the concept of 'need' but stresses the need for love as well as that for iodine and vitamin C, which seems to confuse the two senses of 'need' already referred to. He thinks, however, that the general norm of homeostasis, which usually goes along with the postulation of needs, should be supplemented by that of self-actualization; self-realization, or growth. This would explain more adequately the conduct of 'mature' people which cannot be explained in terms of the tendency to restore an equilibrium state. There are growth needs as well as basic needs.

This is back to Herbert Spencer with a vengeance. Moral philosophers have never been able to make much of the concept of 'self-realization' when it has been used as an over-all end to *justify* actions; to use it as a concept to *explain* them seems scarcely an encouraging move. For the criteria used to specify which sort of self is to be realized involve both personal preferences and cultural requirements. If such

an end is stated with sufficient generality to avoid these
difficulties, it becomes so formal that it is more or less
vacuous. Indeed perhaps the only common denomina-
tor of such postulated end-states would be that they
are states that are commendable, states that we think
people ought to enjoy. Maslow's protest against
deficiency motivation draws attention to such things
as spontaneity, problem-solving, autonomy, de-
tachment and the desire for privacy, freshness of
appreciation, creativeness, and so on. These may well
be ways of referring to common characteristics of
things that are worth doing which are not done out of
necessity, or to remedy an obvious bodily need, or for
some further end. But it is difficult to see how reference
to self-realization *explains* them. For this is merely a
way of classing together things that are, or ought to
be, enjoyed for themselves as distinct from those that
are contingent for their desirability on something else.
The self to be realized will vary according to different
estimates of things that are worth doing for themselves.

III *The return to hedonism*

If 'growth' motivation involves a return to Herbert
Spencer, another alternative to drive-reduction involves a return to Bentham—perhaps even to Aristotle. It
would be none the worse for that if more attention were
paid to the subtlety of some of Aristotle's analyses—
especially his analysis of 'pleasure'. For the main lack
in modern versions of hedonism is one of sophistication
about the concept of 'pleasure'. McClelland admits that
one of his reasons for returning to hedonism is that it

is a common-sense theory about the control of behaviour which is as old as Plato's Protagoras. But this only shows that we use the concept of 'pleasure' in certain contexts; it does not show that it is a particularly useful *explanatory* concept.

McClelland has also been influenced by the inadequacy of need-reduction and strong stimulation theories and impressed by the phenomena of exteroceptively elicited patterns of behaviour already referred to. In particular Young's experiments, which have shown that the palatibility of different sorts of food, as well as their need-reducing properties, have to be reckoned with in explaining eating behaviour, have convinced him that the concept of 'affective arousal' should take the place of that of 'drive'. Any theory, he says, must take account of the active comforts and pleasures of life as well as of discomforts and their relief.

McClelland, so it seems, uses the concept of 'affective arousal', as Hull uses the concept of 'drive', to explain both the acquisition of motives and their activation once acquired. Indeed I have already had occasion in my second chapter to point out that his definition, a variant of which is that a motive is 'a strong affective association, characterized by an anticipatory goal reaction and based on past association of certain cues with pleasure and pain' (McClelland, 1951) makes the conceptual mistake of including a theory about the origin of motives in the definition of 'motive'. His suggestion (McClelland, 1953) is that:

'certain stimuli or situations involving discrepancies between expectation (adaptation level) and perception are sources of primary unlearned affect, either positive or negative in nature. Cues which are paired with these affective states, changes in these affective states, and the conditions producing them become capable of redintegrating a state (A') derived from the original affective situation (A), but not identical with it. To give a simple example, this means that if a buzzer is associated with eating saccharine the buzzer will in time attain the power to evoke a motive or redintegrate a state involving positive affective change. Likewise the buzzer if associated with shock will achieve the power to redintegrate a negative affective state. These redintegrated states, which might be called respectively *appetite* and *anxiety*, are based on the primary affective situation but are not identical with it ' (p. 28).

P. T. Young gives the example of an animal sipping sugar and returning for another sip. A positive affective process aroused by a sweet taste must be assumed. If it receives an electric shock it will tend to avoid the place. A negative affective process must here be assumed.

'In both situations the affective process is inferred as a cause or source of behaviour and as a factor that sustains or terminates the pattern aroused. . . . The acquisition of approach and avoidance patterns proceeds according to the hedonic principle of maximizing positive affectivity (delight, enjoyment) and minimizing negative affectivity (distress). The hedonic processes thus regulate behaviour in a very fundamental sense. They underlie the *direction* that is characteristic of many acquired motives. We have defined motivation as the contemporary process of arousing, sustaining, and channeling behaviour. Affective processes meet all the requirements of this definition. They arouse, sustain, and channel. (Young, 1955).

K

Now this model is the replica of that presented by Bentham and other classical hedonists, though they lacked the physiological patter which goes with it nowadays. But if the postulation of such affective states or hedonic processes, which Young admits to be *an inference*, is to be *explanatory*, they must be defined in a manner which is independent of the description necessary to define the explicandum. They must also be identified by criteria other than those which are necessary to describe the conditions which are assumed to produce them. McClelland realizes this difficulty and tries valiantly to face it. But his criteria do not really seem to meet obvious objections.

He suggests measuring the respiratory rate, the resistance of the skin to an electric current, and other such changes associated with conditional disturbance; but he admits that this will not enable him to distinguish positive from negative affect, only a general increase or decrease in affect. Expressive movements are his next suggestion. This may be a useful guide and perhaps extremes of aversion like disgust can be distinguished, out of context, from extremes of appetite But usually such recognition is almost impossible apart from the sequence of events in which it occurs. Overt expression is obviously, too, very subject to cultural and personal variations. How could one tell, by looking at the face of a man on the way to rob a bank or even to murder his wife, that his motive of greed or jealousy had been activated? He might be very strongly motivated in both cases but might appear as cool as a cucumber. McClelland's next suggestion that verbal behaviour like 'I dislike it', 'I feel good' might also be studied is not very helpful either; for half the problem with hedonism is just to find the correct analysis of such expressions. McClelland turns finally to approach and avoidance behaviour as the best indication. But he admits the seeming circularity of this. For a motive is being explained by reference to affective arousal, and approach and avoidance behaviour (i.e. motivated behaviour) is being used as the criterion for saying that effective arousal has occurred.

McClelland lists some very interesting speculations about the antecedent conditions for affective arousal. He relies on Helson's concept of 'adaptation level' and suggests that positive affect is the result of smaller discrepancies of a perceptual or sensory event from the adaptation level of the organism and that negative affect is the result of larger discrepancies. This discrepancy must persist for a finite length of time before it gives rise to a hedonic response. Changes in adaptation level, with attendant hedonic changes, may be produced by somatic conditions (e.g. hormone cycles in the case of sexual sensations), and they may be produced by experience. Pleasure therefore depends upon a moderate degree of novelty.

These are very interesting assumptions. But the difficulty of distinguishing affective arousal from the conditions that produce it is obvious enough. Indeed McClelland guards himself against having to make the distinction when he says that motives are formed by pairing cues with affective arousal *or* with the conditions that produce it. If a baby chimpanzee has, through experience, a settled expectation of seeing other chimpanzees, it will evince fear if presented with a detached chimpanzee head, although it will evince no such fear reactions before it had formed a

settled expectation of what a chimpanzee should look
like.   The pairing of the cue (the detached head) with
negative affect will set up a motive of fear in relation
to objects of this class. But how can the negative
affect be separated from the conditions which produce it? Is the relationship between these conditions
and negative affect a *causal* relation any more than
negative affect is a *cause* of the subsequent behaviour
of withdrawal from the detached head? Are there two
events—looking at the head and feeling distress?
Surely not; for looking at the head may be distressing,
but there is no separable *sui generis* feeling of distress.

Young admits that the postulation of hedonic
process is an *inference* to explain how a rat comes to
develop an approach motive towards sugar solution
irrespective of its condition of general hunger. He
wants to reject the peripheralist account of this in
terms of S–R connexions favoured by drive reduction theorists. In his theory the postulation of
hedonic processes is a suggestion that there are intervening *central* processes of a different sort which
explain the change in behaviour.

> 'We need concepts like enjoyment, distress, approach
> to satiation, relief, and the like, to describe the facts,
> and we need physiological principles other than those
> relating to the senses, to explain them '.

This is an important and revealing remark. For
though terms like 'pleasure' and 'discomfort' have an
important rôle in *describing* situations, it is doubtful
whether they have an explanatory rôle. Indeed there
is surely no need for Young and McClelland to use
terms like 'pleasure' and 'affective processes' at all in

their explanations. The explanatory work is done by concepts like 'adaptation level' and 'palatability' which correlate antecedent variables with differences in learning and performance.

There can be no objection, either, to his postulation of physiological processes of a central sort which intervene between the presentation of a palatable stimulus and the learned tendency of an animal or human being to seek contact with something similar. Physiological findings like those of Olds on the mechanisms underlying reward are extremely interesting and important. They are not, however, very surprising; for it is a reasonable conjecture that something is going on in the brain or central nervous system in rewarding situations. But it does not seem necessary to introduce reference to 'pleasure' into the explanation, as if it were a special state correlated with such processes.

What then is the explanation of calling a theory 'hedonism' and insisting, at the same time, that the theory is about objective processes 'which can be described as bodily (physical) processes within the tissues of the animal subjects'—especially when the dragging in of pleasure and of affective arousal seems to serve no important explanatory purpose? The answer is surely to be sought in an analysis of how terms like 'pleasure' and 'satisfaction' function, rather than by doing a lot more research. For such an analysis could explain both the insistence that modern theories are a form of hedonism and the failure to make terms like 'pleasure' do any explanatory work. An adequate account of concepts like these would probably occupy another whole monograph. But it is worth while indicating the rough lines along which such an analysis would take in so far as it seems to account for the phenomenon of modern hedonism.

If it is said that a man eats because he enjoys eating or gardens because of the pleasure he gets out of gardening this is a way of *denying* explanations such as that he is eating out of hunger or gardening for a living—i.e. that he has a motive for eating in the usual sense of 'motive'. Such hedonistic descriptions may also indicate that in doing such things a man is absorbed, not easily distracted, not bored, and that these are the sorts of things that he continues to do when the opportunity arises. They are things that are done for their own sake. Now it is significant that the phenomena which have given rise to modern hedonism are monkeys and apes exploring their environment and solving problems for no ulterior motive and rats eating and drinking when they are not hungry or thirsty. To explain such phenomena Nissen's 'drive to know', McClelland's use of the concept of adaptation level, and Young's 'palatability' have come to the fore. Whatever the status of these explanations, they have the common property of being attempts to explain behaviour that is not directed towards any end extrinsic to the action. It is not therefore surprising that they have been thought of as involving hedonic processes. For the reference to pleasure implies that these things are done for their own sake. They are *not* done out of necessity, duty, or for any ulterior motive. Rats sip sugar not because they are hungry; they simply enjoy sipping sugar.

It might be said that this may be true but nevertheless tasting sugar does cause pleasure—a positive and often localized feeling which lasts for a certain time; it is therefore not unreasonable to postulate hedonic processes or states. But is it plausible to analyze what happens in terms of a sweet taste which causes a separate and distinctive feeling of pleasure, or a state of affective arousal? A sweet taste is pleasant; but that does not mean that there are two things, the sweet taste and the pleasure. For how can the so-called 'feeling of pleasure' be regarded as anything distinct from the taste which is described as pleasant? Surely to describe it as pleasant or to say that it causes pleasure is to class it with a whole lot of other things that seem worth experiencing or doing for their own sakes. The pleasure of tasting sugar is specific to tasting sugar; the pleasure of sexual activity is specific to sexual activity; the pleasure of finding out things is specific to finding out things. It is difficult to see what properties the alleged hedonic states have in common if they are thought of as species under a genus. The common meaning in saying that all such experiences are pleasant must surely be conceived of in a different manner.

There may of course be distinctive bodily manifestations and physiological changes that accompany and succeed pleasant sensations like the tasting of sugar or painful ones like receiving an electric shock. These might well be referred to in terms of 'arousal'; but the form of arousal would be specific to the different sorts of pleasures and pains in question and inseparable from the contexts in which they occurred. These may well be used to help to re-formulate the law of effect. Indeed with rats and monkeys there is little alternative as they cannot talk and say things like 'what a pleasant taste' or 'tasting sugar gives me pleasure'. But developing a theory which, as McClelland says, takes account of the active comforts and pleasures of life, does not involve any reference to pleasure as an *explanatory* concept. For hedonism is not an explanatory theory; it is only a way of distinguishing some sorts of sensations and activities from others.

IV 'Intrinsic' regulation

Once it has been seen that to say that one enjoys something or gets pleasure from it does not really *explain* why one tends to do such things, the question can be asked why people enjoy the things which they say that they enjoy. This is an odd question at the common-sense level; for to say that one enjoys doing something is a way of denying that one has a motive for doing it and usually blocks further 'why' questions about it. But there is no reason why one should not investigate the various things that people say that they enjoy doing and see whether any explanation can be given of why they say this about some sorts of things rather than others.

Koch's contribution to the 1956 Nebraska Symposium is very interesting both because he sees the limitations of the usual drive-reduction sort of explanation and because he tries to sketch the direction for a theory to explain things which· people enjoy doing for their own sake. He claims that the extension of what he calls the model of extrinsic regulation is responsible for much of the metaphysics in such ambitious theories. This common-sense model of explanation consists in fitting the behaviour into the

formula 'X does Y in order to . . .' If an easily identifiable referent for the end-term is not available it is
filled in by one that is empty or trivial like 'to be
happy', 'to obtain pleasure', or 'to be peaceful'.
This leads to the classification of drives, wishes,
desires, demands and so on and

> 'the specification of some canonical type of causal system
> to which the "functional properties" of all motives must
> conform (e.g. deficit replacement, tension reduction,
> equilibrium restoral, homeostasis, quiescence-restoral,
> drive-reduction)' (p. 62).

Criterial conditions for the end-state are then postulated—e.g. pleasure, pain, drive-stimulus diminution,
and attempts are made to show that some motives
so classified are fundamental and others are derivative.
Often, however, theorists, no less than common-sense
people, are confronted with cases where there is no
readily identifiable 'extrinsic end'. So recourse is
made to 'irrelevant drive'; or drives like that of
curiosity are invented in an *ad hoc* manner; or the
behaviour is regarded as derivative from a genetically
prior drive; or a genuine exception is admitted by
speaking of 'functional autonomy'.

> 'These scientific theories began with the common-
> sense assumption of conventional "extrinsic" motivation.
> But, curiously enough, one gets the impression that most
> of the energy of the theorists has gone into devizing
> clever accounts for the exceptions to the assumption'
> (p. 64).

Koch's positive suggestion is that 'intrinsically
regulated' behaviour of the 'in and for itself' variety
should be frankly recognized and its characteristics

described; that it should be realized that a great many activities—lowly ones like going to the movies or driving a fast car, as well as the more exalted ones like creative thinking—are instances of it; and a positive theory of value-determining properties of such activities should be developed. This would accord well with the recent findings on exploratory and manipulation drives.

> 'If less time were spent postulating new drive systems and more time devoted, say, to narrowing down the range of characters which cause monkeys to "solve" some manipulative problems and not others, this would truly put us on the track of facts required by an "intrinsic grammar". If more effort, say, were devoted not to whether increased stimulation can "reinforce", but to what the detailed properties might be of those "stimulus" increases which *do* reinforce, psychology might find itself at a new threshold' (p. 82).

Koch's attack on 'extrinsic regulation' is so much in line with the general thesis of this monograph that it deserves one or two comments. The first and obvious point is that his attack on 'extrinsic regulation' endangers the baby as well as the bath-water. He does not bring out clearly that reference to end-states like drive-reduction or homeostasis are logically inappropriate completions to the formula 'X does Y in order to . . .' A man does not enter a restaurant in order to relieve his tension. He does so in order to eat. He does not usually eat either in order to relieve his tensions, though eating may in fact do something like this. Koch does not make anything of the distinction between 'goal' and 'end-state' and of the different levels of question which are answered by reference to them. *At the proper level,* the completion of the formula 'X does Y in order to . . .' is the only appropriate answer to some versions of the question 'Why does X do Y?' The postulation of unconscious motives is, too, a very good answer to other versions of the question—e.g. 'What made X do Y?' The fact that these answers are given by common-sense is no objection to them; indeed it is one of the points in their favour.

But he does see, like philosophers from Aristotle to G. E. Moore, that there are some activities of which it makes no further sense to say 'What is the point of doing X?' He also sees that to explain them in terms of the reduction of some nebulous drive is metaphysical—i.e. an empty extension of a limited explanatory model. Whether his own positive suggestion that their value-determining properties should be studied in order to develop a different sort of theory is likely to be fruitful is another matter. For could this ever be an *explanation* of such activities as distinct from a more detailed *description* of their characteristics? Koch stresses that he is merely giving a direction for theorizing, not a theory. So perhaps it is premature to assess his positive suggestion.

CHAPTER SIX

CONCLUSION

A MONOGRAPH must necessarily be more
like a missionary enterprise than a full-scale
deployment of resources. It is selective in its approach
and limited in its scale of operations. The most
that can be hoped for is that there will be a cross-
fertilization between established traditions and the
ideas that are critical of them. The aim of this monograph has been to contribute to the development of
theories of motivation by subjecting some leading
examples of contemporary theories to conceptual
analysis. For it is my conviction that conceptual
confusion is one of the main causes of the present
unsatisfactory state in motivational psychology.

There is one main tradition which has been repeatedly criticized in this monograph—the tradition
stemming from Hobbes that there can be an all-
inclusive theory of human behaviour from whose
basic postulates answers to all forms of the questions
'Why does Jones do X?' will eventually be deduced.
Such theories are usually known as theories of motivation. It has been stressed that there are many particular forms of the general question 'Why does Jones
do X?' and that answers to them are logically different
and sometimes logically exclusive. Ambitious theories
of motivation tend to take models of explanation that

are appropriate to answering some forms of 'why' questions and to generalize them to answer quite different forms.

The most obvious and usual answer to the question 'Why' about human actions is to find the goal or end towards which an action is directed or the rule to which the action is made to conform. This is the paradigm case of a human action—when a man has a reason for doing something. In our own society we are familiar with most of the possible goals and conventions which might be relevant. The explanatory task is to find which one is operative on a particular occasion. The job of anthropologists and sociologists, to a large extent, is to exhibit the structure of goals and conventions in unfamiliar societies. For this is the most obvious way of making human actions intelligible—classifying them as actions of a certain sort. There are, of course, *further questions* about actions which are of interest to psychologists as well as to social scientists. There are, for instance, questions about how these rules are passed on, the conditions which favour the pursuit of some goals rather than others, individual differences in the pursuit of goals, and the factors which determine variations in the persistence with which they are pursued. There are also questions about deviations from prescribed patterns of rules and goal-seeking, and the factors—e.g. in childhood—which influence the development of unusual or substitute goals. In fact a host of questions dealt with by theories like that of Freud's infantile sexuality and learning theories. But classification of the main types of goals and conventions must surely be the preliminary job of anyone interested in explaining human actions. That is why McDougall, though in his theory of instincts he made the common mistake of translating a conceptual insight into a genetic theory, was much more on the right lines than many modern theorists of motivation. For he stressed the irreducibility of 'purpose', classified the major goals of men, and developed some useful tools of description. For instance his principles of 'conative unity' and 'conative persistence' were important in stressing the way acts over a period are to be explained in terms of some over-riding goal. His distinction, too, between 'tastes' and 'sentiments' was conceptually important.

McDougall, too, like his more methodologically sophisticated follower, Tolman, insisted that purposive behaviour was irreducible. Descriptions of it could not be deduced from higher level theories of a mechanical type. Indeed, McDougall really pushed the purposive model too far; for at times he seemed to credit even the lower animals with unsuspected powers of foresight and adaptability. But he did agree with the main thesis of this monograph—that explanations of the purposive, rule-following type, occupy a sort of logical ceiling in explaining human actions. They cannot be *deduced* from more general postulates of a mechanical type as envisaged by Hobbes, Hull, and perhaps Freud in his more speculative physiological moments.

This, of course, does not mean that there is no place for causal theories of a mechanical type in psychology. There are occasions when actions break down or are disrupted when explanations of this type are required. If we ask what *made* Jones eat his hat or what made him mistake the name of his best friend or bungle a familiar performance, a theory of this type is extremely apposite. It may be a theory of a physiological sort or in terms of stimulation or 'unconscious wishes'. Freud claimed that he had advanced explanations of a psychological type in terms of 'wishes' into a sphere where previously only physiological explanations had been given. And certainly, for those interested in such causal explanations, it is a most important question to decide what sorts of cases—e.g. different types of paralysis—are to be explained physiologically and what sorts require an explanation of the Freudian type. But, as has been repeatedly stressed, Freudian explanations of this type only explain what *happens* to a man. His account of what a man *does*, in terms of ego-functions, is logically quite different. It is, in fact, simply making explicit the rule-following purposive model.

In theories of motivation, in addition to purposive rule-following explanations, and those in terms of efficient causes, there are also to be found all-inclusive explanations in terms of concepts like 'need reduction', 'homeostasis', 'satisfaction', and so on. It has been pointed out that these are answers to higher-level types of question and that they often seem to be normative justifications masquerading as all-inclusive explanations. Hedonism, which has been recently revived, is a case in point. The view has been strenuously resisted that there is a deductive relationship between some such very general homeostatic postulate and lower-level postulates of a causal or purposive type.

There is a further very important logical consideration which makes all-inclusive theories of motivation

inappropriate. It has been argued that the term
'motive' is used predominantly in contexts where
there is a breakdown in conventional expectations,
when a man acts 'out of character', and that it points
to the goal towards which his behaviour is actually
directed. It is unlike explanations in terms of the rule-
following purposive model because it is required when
the behaviour seems to be goal-directed but to conform to no established rules. This explains the frequent
connexion of postulates of motivation in psychology
with learning and experimental situations. Indeed
there is some point in Allport's rather cryptic remark
that motives are habits in the making. For certainly
to ask for a person's motive rules out the suggestion
that he might be acting out of habit. The notion of
goal-directedness without any set pattern of reaching
the goal is also characteristic of the Freudian 'wish'.
Perhaps this is why Freud's theory is most usually
quoted as a theory of 'motives'. But to explain
everything a man does in terms of 'motives' is logically
inappropriate because it lumps together acting
purposefully according to rules, acting with a goal
but according to no established rules, and cases where
something happens to a man and it is odd to say that
he *acts* at all. Psychologists, therefore, who say that all
behaviour is motivated are using the concept too
widely if by this they mean that we have a motive for
everything we do.

But, they may not mean this. For, as has been
pointed out, such a shift has occurred in the use of
the term 'motive' in America that, for some psychologists, 'motives' have become more or less synonymous
with 'drives' and no longer imply directedness; they

saying that a concept used in one model of
explanation is inapplicable in another; cannot deduce
CONCLUSION   the one from the   153   other.

are, indeed, contrasted with steering terms like
'habit' and 'reaction-tendency'. Furthermore, theories
of motivation are usually not theories about what
motives must be postulated in order to explain what
people do; rather they are theories about the conditions which facilitate the learning and performance
of rats. Drive theories, to repeat, do not seem to be
explanations in terms of goal-directedness; rather
they are explanations *of* variations in persistence
towards goals and the activation and stamping in of
some habits rather than others. Theories of 'needs',
too, are ambiguous in the same sort of way. For
sometimes they provide classifications of behaviour
in terms of socially approved goals; at other times
recourse is made to 'needs' to *explain* such goal-
directed sequences, as when drinking is explained by
the need of the body to preserve a constant amount of
liquid. It has been argued that the latter sort of theory
is useful in answering certain limited questions—
usually about the body—but that it becomes metaphysical and ambiguous when generalized, in that it
confuses the above two senses of 'need', and also
confuses explanation with normative recommenda-
tion. Over and over again, in the field of motivation,
it has been shown that there is conceptual confusion.
Plenty of facts are known—e.g. those connected with
palatability or with infantile sexuality—but they are
thought to confirm empty over-all theories like homeostasis or hedonism.

I started off by comparing a monograph with a
missionary enterprise. It might well be said, however,
that this monograph is more like an underground
movement. It delivers thrusts at the established order

L

in psychology from within, but never comes above ground to make any positive suggestions. But there is surely no need to make explicit what is implicit in the whole thesis—that different and logically appropriate theories should be developed to answer different sorts of questions rather than all-inclusive theories to answer all of them. Theories, for instance, about the mechanisms underlying behaviour should not be mistaken for sufficient explanations of behaviour. Theories which employ concepts like that of 'motive' or 'wish' should be distinguished from theories *of* motivation which employ concepts such as that of 'drive', 'need', or 'sensitization'. All such different theories should not be lumped together under an all-inclusive theory employing a concept with a very limited application like that of 'stimulation'.

It might well be objected that psychologists use terms like 'drive', 'need', and 'motive' in a technical sense and that, provided that they give their own rules for using the term, it does not matter much what term they choose. In my view it would be a profound mistake for psychologists to take such a cavalier attitude towards ordinary speech. For the different terms employed by ordinary educated people incorporate distinctions which may be unwarrantably ignored by theorists. Drive theorists, for instance, use the term 'drive' in such a way that a man can have a hunger drive, a drive to play poker rather than tennis, a drive to repeat acts in a compulsive manner, and even a drive to know. Now surely this leads to confusion. For apart from the fact that it is logically absurd to say that one could be driven to know anything, the use of the same term for all these very different types

all is saying is that one
model maker more distinctions than
another. (Has to justify the distinction >>>)
CONCLUSION   155
                                           see below
                                             ↓

of action, is a case of unwarrantable assimilation in the
interest of an over-all theory. Ordinary language
would only use the term 'drive' in the case of compulsive repetition and, perhaps, in cases of extreme
hunger, as when a man eats his hat. This is no accident;
it is not a matter merely of terminology. For there
are very important distinctions between the types of
behaviour in question. In cases like this, ordinary
language, by being specific in its employment of a
concept, singles out differences in behaviour which are
theoretically as well as practically important. Would
it not be better, therefore, for psychologists to confine
a concept like that of 'drive' to cases where, in ordinary
language, a man could properly be said to be 'driven'
to act? The difficulty about developing a science of
psychology is that, in a sense, we already know too
much about human behaviour, albeit in a rather unco-
ordinated manner. Common-sense, which is incorporated in the concepts of ordinary language, has
creamed off most of the vital distinctions. Psychology
has the task of systematizing what is already known
and adding bits of special theory to supplement
common-sense, e.g. Freudian theory and theories
about conditions which facilitate learning. If it dis-
penses with terms such as 'motive' it has at least to
show that the conceptual scheme which it develops
instead can take care of crucial distinctions made by
common-sense. Given an appropriate set of concepts
for the classification of behaviour falling within the
purposive, rule-following model, concepts like that of
'drive', 'motive', 'instinct', and 'need' would find their
place as supplementary concepts for explaining particular sorts of departures from this model; or for

answering higher level questions about the conditions which facilitate and hinder learning such goal-directed sequences and which account for individual differences in goal-directedness. Physiological psychology, too, would come into its own not as a higher level theory from which descriptions of behaviour could be deduced, but as a theory about some of the necessary conditions of behaviour and of the sufficient conditions for some sorts of individual differences and breakdowns in performance.

In brief, the rule-following purposive model is basic in explaining human behaviour. A lot of work needs to be done, as it is hoped this monograph has shown, in clarifying some of the concepts which it employs and which are auxiliary to it. Its content, too, needs to be filled in for each particular society with the help of anthropologists and sociologists. The descriptions and explanations which it employs cannot be deduced from higher level theories of a logically dissimilar type. But they need to be supplemented by auxiliary theories taken from disciplines like physiology, drive psychology, and Freudian theory. In this way all those interested in motivation, psychologists and philosophers alike, can work together in a more piecemeal and tolerant manner. For toleration will surely follow the acceptance of the thesis that the role of the Galileo of psychology must be for ever unoccupied. Psychology has not soared into its Galilean period as is often thought, through lack of bright ideas, experimental ingenuity, or methodological rigour. It has remained earth-bound in mazes and Skinner boxes because the highly general theories which, it was hoped, would emerge, are *logically* impossible. The fundamental mistake of theorists like Lewin and Hull was to assume that what psychology requires is a Galileo. What would be much more salutary would be a more careful scrutiny of the conceptually illuminating start made by Aristotle.

BIBLIOGRAPHY

ALLPORT, G. W. (1937) 'The Functional Autonomy of Motives', *American Journal of Psychology*, **50,** p. 154.

BENTHAM, J. (1879) *Principles of Morals and Legislation*, Oxford, Clarendon Press, p. 99 (reprint of A New Edition published by Bentham in 1823).

BROWN, J. S. (1953) 'Problems Presented by the Concept of Acquired Drive', *Current Theory and Research in Motivation*, University of Nebraska Press.

DOLLARD, J. and MILLER, N. E. (1950), *Personality and Psychotherapy*, McGraw Hill, New York, p. 80.

FARBER, I. G. (1954), 'Anxiety as a Drive State', *Nebraska Symposium on Motivation*.

FREUD, S. (1914) *The Psychopathology of Everyday Life*, Ernest Benn, London, pp. 192-3.

FREUD, S. (1922) *Beyond the Pleasure Principle*, Hogarth Press, London, pp. 1, 2.

FREUD, S. (1935) *Collected Papers* Vol. IV, Hogarth Press, London, pp. 62-6.

FREUD, S. (1927) *The Ego and the Id*, Hogarth Press, London, p. 30.

FREUD, S. (1949) *An Outline of Psycho-analysis*, Hogarth Press, London, pp. 24-31.

FREUD, S. (1950) *Collected Papers*, Vol. V, Hogarth Press, p. 127.

FREUD, S. (1955) *Collected Papers*, Vol. XIII, Hogarth Press, London, p. 166.

GUTHRIE, E. R. and HORTON, E. P. (1946) *Cats in a Puzzle Box*, Rinehart, New York.

HAMLYN, D. W. (1953) 'Behaviour', *Philosophy*, **28** pp. 132-145.

(1957) *The Psychology of Perception*, Routledge and Kegan Paul, London.

HARLOW, H. (1953), 'Mice, Monkeys, Men, and Motives', *Psychological Review*, **60**, pp. 23-32.

(1953a) 'Motivation as a Factor in the Acquisition of New Responses', *Current Theory and Research in Motivation*.

HEBB, D. O. (1949) *The Organization of Behaviour*, Wiley, London, p. 181.

HULL, C. L. (1943) *The Principles of Behaviour*, Appleton-Century-Crofts, New York, pp. 25-6.

JONES, E. (1954) *Sigmund Freud, Life and Work*, Vol. I, Hogarth Press, London, p. 436.

JONES, E. (1955) *Sigmund Freud, Life and Work*, Vol. II, Hogarth Press, London, p. 350.

KOCH, S. (1954) ' Clark L. Hull', in *Modern Learning Theory*, Appleton-Century-Crofts, New York, pp. 22-51.

KOCH, S. (1956) 'Behaviour as "intrinsically" regulated ', *Nebraska Symposium on Motivation*.

MCCLELLAND, D. C. (1951) *Personality*, Sloane, New York, p. 466.

(1953) *The Achievement Motive*, Appleton-Century-Crofts, New York, p. 28.

MCCLELLAND, D. C. (1955) *Studies in Motivation*, Appleton-Century-Crofts, New York.

MCDOUGALL, W. (1928) *Outline of Psychology*, Methuen, London. (Revised Ed.)

MCGUINESS, B. F. (1957) 'I know what I Want', *Proc. Aristot. Soc.*, May.

MASLOW, A (1955) 'Deficiency Motivation and Growth Motivation', *Nebraska Symposium on Motivation*, p. 5.

MORGAN, C T and STELLAR, E (1950) *Physiological Psychology*, McGraw Hill, Ch. 18.

MURRAY, H. A. (1938) *Explorations in Personality*, Oxford University Press, Ch. 2.

NEWCOMB, T. H. (1950) *Social Psychology*, The Dryden Press, New York, pp. 80, 81.

NISSEN, H. W. (1954) 'The Nature of the Drive as Innate Determinant of Behaviour Organization', *Nebraska Symposium on Motivation*, pp. 308, 9.

OLDS, J. (1955) 'Physiological Mechanisms of Reward', *Nebraska Symposium on Motivation*.

PETERS, R. S. (1951) 'Observationalism in Psychology', *Mind*, **60**, January.

(1952) 'Motives and Causes', *Proc. Aristot. Soc.* Supp. **26**, pp. 146-147, 156.

PETERS, R. S. (1956) 'Motives and Motivation', *Philosophy*, **31**, pp. 117–120.

PETERS, R. S. (1956) *Hobbes*, Penguin Books, pp. 91-7.

PETERS, R. S. (1957) and TAJFEL, H. 'Hobbes and Hull, Metaphysicians of Behaviour', *Brit. Philosophy of Science*, May, pp. 36-40..

PIAGET, J. (1932) *The Moral Judgement of the Child*, Kegan Paul, London.

POPPER, K. R. (1945) *The Open Society and Its Enemies*, Vol. 11, Kegan Paul, London, p. 90.

RYLE, G. (1949) *The Concept of Mind*, Hutchinson, London, Ch. 4.

STAGNER, R. and KARWOSKI, T. F. (1952) *Psychology*, McGraw Hill, New York, p. 39.

SKINNER, B. F. (1938) *The Behaviour of Organisms*, Appleton-Century-Crofts, New York.

TOLMAN, E. C. (1932) *Purposive Behaviour in Animals and Men*, Appleton-Century-Crofts, New York.

TOLMAN, E. C. (1938) 'The Determiners of Behaviour at a Choice Point', *Psychological Review*, **45**; 1-41.

URMSON, J. O. (1952) 'Motives and Causes, *Proc. Aristoc. Soc.*, *Supp.*, **26**;, pp. 179-184.

WHITE, A. R. (1958) 'The Language of Motives', *Mind*, **67**, pp. 258–263.

WITTGENSTEIN, L. (1953) *Philosophical Investigations*, Blackwell, Oxford, p. 174.

YOUNG, P. T. (1955) 'The Role of Hedonic Processes in Motivation', *Nebraska Symposium on Motivation*, p. 194.

INDEX

Some behavior "priced" when not aware of it.

[?]

What Rogers is talking about is not talking of "motives" and "motivation" but recognising what people want to do for own sake.

149   main part of monograph

Maxwell : Analysis of
          Qualitative Data

Snedecor & Cochran : Statistical
          Methods
          1966

S.v.R.
30, Elwood Rd,
    Bradway,
    Sheffield.

35, Edgwarebury Gdns,
    Edgware,
    M.D.D X.